# The Science of Love

Glenn D. Wilson & Chris McLaughlin

First published in Great Britain in 2001 by Fusion Press, a
division of Satin Publications Ltd.

Reprinted 2001

This book is copyright under the Berne convention. All rights reserved.
No part of this publication may be reproduced, stored in a retrieval
system, or transmitted in any form or by any means, electronic,
mechanical, photocopying, recording or otherwise, without prior
written permission of the publisher.

© 2001 Glenn D. Wilson and Chris McLaughlin

Fusion Press
101 Southwark Street
London SE1 0JH
UK
e-mail: info@visionpaperbacks.co.uk
website: www.visionpaperbacks.co.uk

Publisher: Sheena Dewan
Cover design © 2001 Nickolai Globe
Typeset by FiSH Books, London
Printed and bound in the UK by Biddles Ltd.

ISBN: 1-901250-54-7

# Contents

# Preface

Science and love might seem unsuitable bedfellows. Science is cold, analytical and objective, while love is warm, cuddly and mysterious. Indeed, this may be why scientists left the topic to poets and philosophers for so many centuries. But in the last few decades there has been a great deal of interest in applying sciences like psychology and neurochemistry to the understanding of human attraction, romantic love and marital success or failure. This book is intended to give the general reader something of the flavour of this scientific research and to outline some of its most exciting findings. We hope that people will find it intriguing as well as helpful in understanding their own feelings and relationships.

The scientific approach is indeed cold in one particular respect. It seeks truth and lets the facts speak for themselves, even if they are sometimes discomforting. People did not want to be told that the Earth is not the centre of the universe or that we have ancestors in common with apes. Likewise, some people may be unhappy with some of the major themes emerging in this book. We have been unable to escape the fact that much of our behaviour in the domain of mating and dating is irrational in that it is driven by hormones, brain chemistry and instincts that have evolved over many millennia and that are shared with other animals. We have also had to accept that men and women are basically different as regards their needs, preferences, motives and personality. Furthermore, these differences are mostly fundamental and biological, not fully accounted for by social role-learning or tradition. Sometimes they seem to propel us towards inevitable conflict in our relations with the opposite sex. Still, we are better to recognise and understand these differences than sweep them under the carpet and pretend they don't exist.

Often these instincts operate outside our awareness, leaving us to rationalise our behaviour in ways that are mentally comforting. Rather than say, 'My libido is pushing me towards sexual novelty and promiscuity, the better to promulgate my genes', a man is more likely to say, 'My wife doesn't understand me'. Rather than say, 'I am being cautioned by brain modules intent on ensuring that my offspring will be well provided for', a woman will say, 'I am saving myself for the one I love'. Our primary purpose is not to strip away these façades but to give readers some deeper insights into the true causes of their behaviour. If differences like this are indeed determined by deep-seated instincts they will not be dissolved by recent changes like the availability of effective contraception or moves towards the political equality of women.

Some people complain that science only endorses common sense. But this is not so. Everyone 'knew' the world was flat until they realised you could sail around it. Historically, most people thought that emotions were felt in the heart, but we now know they stem from processes occurring in the brain. Moreover, common sense likes to have it all ways. 'Absence makes the heart grow fonder' rings a bell with most people, but so does 'out of sight, out of mind'. It is the job of science to decide which proverb is true and which false, or more likely, under what conditions and for what sort of people each applies. For example, introverts might be inclined to pine for a lost lover, while extraverts rapidly find a new partner.

For science, what ultimately counts is that ideas are put to the test and survive. Sigmund Freud's insights are not necessarily any more valuable than Bill Bloggs's opinions. No authority is so impressive that their ideas are beyond the need for verification. Speculation is permissible, and will be indulged in from time to time throughout this book, but it is important that it be recognised as such and abandoned or modified as soon as evidence requires.

We hope that this book will help to unravel some of the mysteries of love and to account for its two sides, the agony and the ecstasy. For 'love hurts' but it also 'conquers all'. It may be, to quote Somerset Maugham, just a 'dirty trick played on us to achieve continuation of the species' but it certainly feels like more than that, and that feeling is important in its own right. Many people would say that, above all else, it is love that makes life worth living, that 'makes the world go round'. The book that follows is concerned with understanding the experience of being in love, as well as the sometimes extraordinary behaviour associated with that state.

Glenn D. Wilson and Chris McLaughlin
London, February 2001

# 1

# Illusion and reality

*Love is like the wind stirring the grass beneath trees on a black night.*
*You must not try to make love definite.*
*It is the divine accident of life.*

Sherwood Anderson[1]

When the Prince of Wales announced his engagement to Lady Diana Spencer in 1980, the reporters wanted to know whether they were in love. 'Yes, whatever that means,' he replied, and was much mocked in the ensuing newspaper stories for his lack of romance. Yet it is a perfectly reasonable comment that deserves – and has received – proper consideration from researchers trying to understand this expression, which we all bandy around so easily. What do we actually mean when we say we are 'in love'? Is it different from simply loving someone? Is it a sound basis on which to build a long-term, satisfying relationship between two people?

## Who wants to know?

Love may have been the favourite topic for poets, novelists and playwrights for centuries, and more recently for cinema and TV, but it is only in the last 50 years that psychologists and social scientists have begun to explore the 'science of love'. Their early studies and experiments were questioned by some who felt that they were wrong to turn the spotlight of scientific investigation on to such a delicate and mysterious aspect of human experience. In the late 1970s, US Senator William Proxmire spoke for many ordinary people when he voiced his reservations about this comparatively new field of research: 'I believe that some 200 million Americans want to leave some things in life a mystery,' he said, 'and right at the top of the list of things we don't want to know is why a man falls in love with a woman, and vice versa.' Yet, as with research into other controversial areas, such as genetics and nuclear physics, the genie, once out of the bottle, cannot be put back.

While the scientific study of love has continued to develop and expand, it is interesting to note that some of those most directly involved – couples whose relationships were put under the microscope by the first researchers – shared the senator's doubts. Psychologist Zick Rubin, a pioneer in this field, noted that some research subjects felt their relationships had been damaged by their participation in studies conducted by himself and his colleagues. 'In some cases, the research cemented relationships; in other cases, it hastened their demise. A few of our participants came to feel that our statistical approach to love demeaned their relationships.'[2] Unlike many of his colleagues, who refused to accept that their critics might have a valid point, Rubin acknowledges the potentially destructive impact of research into love. 'Rather than sticking with a partner for better or worse,' he suggests, 'men and women came to believe that a marriage should survive only if love – and with it, individual fulfilment – continued to flower.'

Will research on love reinforce this trend of questioning – and toppling – existing relationships? And is such questioning of people's closest ties to be welcomed or to be shunned? This question is probably unanswerable in practice and, in any case, the desire to understand human love is so powerful, both among researchers and the general public, that it will continue to be studied, regardless of any possible negative consequences.

# Defining 'love'

One of the major obstacles when it comes to analysing love is that we use the word very loosely, even though it describes many very different experiences and emotions. Much time and effort has been – and still is – devoted by researchers to attempting to devise meaningful definitions and to distinguish between different kinds of love. In his early work in the field, Rubin tried to pinpoint what people meant when they said they 'loved' someone.[3] His findings demonstrated that it didn't necessarily involve 'liking' them. On the basis of couples' replies to questionnaires, he concluded that loving and liking evoke distinct responses and types of behaviour and, although they may overlap, they don't always. He devised a scale that reflected the differences in the way his subjects felt about their friends and the person they said they loved (see Table 1.1). His findings confirmed what many of us know from experience: you can think very highly of another person, have warm feelings towards them and enjoy their company without loving them. Loving, according to Professor Rubin's study, has three essential components: attachment, caring and intimacy. By attachment, he meant wanting to be with the other person as much as possible and receiving emotional support from them. Caring for someone means being as concerned about their well-being as about your own – or even more, while intimacy implies a close bond and sharing your thoughts and feelings in a way you would not do with other people.

Table 1.1 Examples of items from Rubin's scales (from Rubin, 1970)

**Liking**
Favourable evaluation
I think that John/Mary is unusually well-adjusted
It seems to me that it is very easy for John/Mary to gain admiration

Respect and confidence
I have great confidence in John/Mary's good judgement
I would vote for John/Mary in a class or group election

Perceived similarity
I think that John/Mary and I are quite similar to each other
When I am with John/Mary, we are almost always in the same mood

**Loving**
Attachment
If I could never be with John/Mary, I would feel miserable
It would be hard for me to get along without John/Mary

Caring
If John/Mary were feeling badly, my first duty would be to cheer him/her up
I would do almost anything for John/Mary

Intimacy
I feel that I can confide in John/Mary about virtually everything
When I am with John/Mary, I spend a good deal of time just looking at him/her

Couples who scored high on this 'love scale' revealed their feelings through their body language. In particular, they spent a lot of time gazing into one another's eyes – much more than couples with lower scores or those who said they were simply friends. They were also likely to sit and stand closer together, and to discourage other people from intruding on their intimacy by turning their bodies towards each other and erecting 'barriers' with their arms and shoulders. Most people can read this kind of signal easily; even if you were not consciously aware that you were being excluded by a couple behaving in this way, you would almost certainly respond by acceding to their unspoken wishes and leaving them alone.

This absorption in one another leads on to other aspects of

love or, perhaps more accurately, of being 'in love' not accounted for in this analysis: what singer-songwriter Joni Mitchell once described as 'the dizzy, dancing way you feel' in her song *Both Sides Now*. The early stages of a romantic relationship can often leave participants on a confusing, uncontrollable roller-coaster of intense emotion – ecstatic one minute and desolate the next – which may be as painful as it is pleasurable. Noel Coward once referred to this state as a kind of 'flu of the heart', and many of those who have experienced it would agree that it can feel like a sickness at times. What's more, it may lead people to behave in ways that they would normally consider risky and undesirable. One study at the University of East Carolina found that over half the students surveyed admitted to various kinds of dangerous behaviour 'in the name of love'[4]: having unsafe sex, giving up aspects of their personality, deceiving their parents and driving under the influence of alcohol or in poor weather conditions. A minority of people take these behaviour changes to extremes, and appear to be prepared to sacrifice whatever it takes – career, family relationships and individual identity – for the sake of love.[5]

With respect to the question posed by Prince Charles, the most pertinent study is that of German psychologists Helmut Lamm and Ulrich Weissmann.[6] They had students write down how they could tell whether they *liked* someone, *loved* someone or were *in love* with someone. Their findings suggested that the most distinctive characteristic of liking someone was the desire to be with them, of love, trust in the other and of being in love, arousal. In other words, it is the emotional turmoil that defines being 'in love' and that separates this condition from both liking and loving.

Psychologists Ellen Berscheid and Elaine Walster coined the term 'passionate love' to distinguish this volatile state from a steadier, more settled emotion that they called 'companionate love'.[7] Apart from its sheer intensity, the main features of passionate love are a disconcerting combination of the positive and the negative – euphoria, excitement, physical arousal, joy and sexual pleasure shadowed by anxiety, jealousy, uncertainty, pain and disappointment. Love like this frequently dominates a person's whole existence, at least for a time, leaving little energy for or interest in other aspects of everyday life. It is perhaps as well, therefore, that passionate love tends not to last; it either dies entirely or is transformed into a less intense but more sustainable form of love.

Dorothy Tennov describes a type of love she calls 'limerence', which is similar to passionate love in that it seems to come out of the blue and take over the person's whole existence.[8] Because it appears to be uncontrollable and often very painful, limerence shares many of the qualities that Lee ascribes to manic love: it is often directed at a person who will never reciprocate in the way the individual wants them to. Such a relationship is almost bound to fail. According to Tennov, women are more prone to experiencing this kind of unsatisfactory love than men.

Companionate love, as distinct from passionate love, gains in longevity what it loses in intensity. This type of lover does not feel the need to concentrate their whole being on the other person, but is able to leave room in their life for other relationships and activities. Sex does not play the dominant role that it does in passionate love (although it may still be very important), but other elements are of equal or greater significance. Affectionate friendship, a true understanding of the other person and the ability to trust them completely are the bedrock of this kind of love. Companionate love, while it may be less exciting and dramatic than passionate love, is more stable and less fragile, and has a better chance of surviving through bad times as well as good.

## *The rose-coloured spectacles effect*

Part of the explanation for the relatively short-lived nature of passionate love may lie in the fact that it is often based on a distorted perception of the 'love object'. That is to say, we fall in love with an idealised version of the other person, the person we believe (and want) them to be, rather than the person they really are. This illusion cannot be sustained as we get to know the other person better and, as inevitably happens, they reveal aspects of themselves that do not fit the idealised image we have created. American psychologist Malcolm Brenner performed a simple experiment that neatly demonstrated this perceptual distortion. He asked young couples to watch a series of activities performed in turn by their partner and by a stranger. When questioned afterwards, they were able to remember the performance of the stranger with fewer distortions than that of their partner. The more in love they were, the greater the distortion of memory.[9]

Many psychologists would make a distinction between passionate love and infatuation. Falling in love with someone who doesn't know you exist or doesn't return your feelings may be a common theme in popular songs, but it is not to be equated with the shared experience of passionate love, however short-lived that relationship may turn out to be. Psychotherapist Nathaniel Brandon has spelled out the difference as he sees it:

> Infatuation differs from love precisely in that, whereas love embraces the person as a whole, infatuation is the result of focusing on one or two traits or aspects and reacting as if that were the total. I see a beautiful face, for example, and imagine it is the image of a beautiful soul. I see how kindly this person treats me and assume we share significant affinities. I discover we share important values in one area and expand this to include the whole of life.[10]

# The colours of love

Some psychologists have gone beyond the dual categorisation of passionate love versus companionate love, and attempted to distinguish several different types of love. Canadian sociologist John Lee, for example, has envisaged six distinct categories, although individuals may well experience love that overlaps the borders between them.[11] Lee uses the analogy of colour to explain his analysis of the types of love: there is no such thing as the ideal or perfect colour, he points out, just the one that is your personal favourite. Similarly, different individuals may prefer different styles of love and, in some instances, their preferences may change over time. Thus he divides his 'love styles' into 'primary' and 'secondary' colours of love, pointing out that blends based on the three primaries can produce an infinite variety of secondary love styles, just as they can with colours. Lee's three primary colours of love, corresponding loosely with red, blue and yellow, are termed Eros, Storge and Ludus.

*Eros* (named after the God of Love) is triggered primarily by the other person's physical characteristics – an erotic lover knows just what sort of looks attract them and home in on that person without hesitation. They want to know everything about their lover and to have an intense sexual relationship with them. Finding the 'right' relationship is an important priority in their lives and, although they want it to be one-to-one, they are not particularly prone to jealousy or possessiveness.

*Ludus* (from the Latin word for 'game' or play') is so named because its adherents regard love primarily as fun and not as a serious business. They are not looking for commitment and may be attracted to a wide range of different people, sometimes at the same time. Such individuals are not prone to falling in love, and tend to shy away from partners who want to get too deeply involved or who are jealous or possessive.

*Storge* (the ancient Greek word for 'affection') is a kind of love that grows slowly over time. It is based on shared activities and interests and profound friendship. Fireworks and drama do not feature in this kind of love, which does not require frequent verbal expression and does not need to be questioned or examined.

The secondary colours of love, according to Lee, are Mania, Pragma and Agape.

*Mania* is a kind of love that is extremely intense, often obsessive, and which must be continually bolstered by reassurance and constant attention. The manic lover may not even like their partner very much, and often falls for the 'wrong' person because they do not see them as they really are. The manic lover's deep need for their partner's love means that they suffer badly from jealousy and their relationships are frequently difficult and painful.

*Pragma* is, as you would expect, love based on pragmatism (practical considerations). The pragmatic lover looks for a partner who will be compatible in terms of shared interests, lifestyle and aspirations. Their love is never based on uncontrollable passion or 'chemistry'. This type of lover tends to advance slowly, making sure that a prospective partner fits the 'template' they have designed before committing themselves. They are most likely to look for their ideal in groups of like-minded people, such as shared-interest clubs or, these days, through computer dating or similar approaches where information about prospective partners is available in advance.

*Agape* (Greek for brotherly love) is, according to Lee, the rarest type of love, at least in human partnerships. It is defined as a selfless, giving kind of love, which is not dependent on profound emotion or sexual desire, and requires love to be given altruistically to the person who needs it. It is the kind of love shown by the Good Samaritan in the Biblical parable. People whose lover is of this type may find themselves sharing his or her time and emotional energy with many other people.

Although a variety of questionnaires and other 'tests' have been devised in attempts to identify which type of love individuals prefer, none has been particularly successful. Lee himself recommends analysing past relationships to see where you fit best. What's more, he also identifies various combinations – such as Storgic Eros, Ludic Eros and Storgic Ludus – which mix some features from the different primaries.

The chart below illustrates how the various categories are related to each other and shows how the different types are presumed to combine in a relationship – whether successfully or otherwise. If two potential lovers each identify their style on this chart, their relationship is more likely to work the nearer to each other they appear on it. Lee calls this the rule of proximity. The match may be either around the perimeter of the circle or across the points of the triangles. Those directly opposite one another are the least compatible pairings.

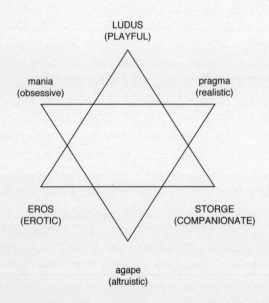

Figure 1.1  Lee's typology of love (from Lee, 1976)

Lee's analysis has been the basis of much subsequent research, but it is by no means universally accepted. Some psychologists, for example, argue that what he calls Ludus is not love at all but merely flirtation, while Storge would be better described as friendship and Mania as a form of neurosis. We return to the question of how best to clarify love styles in Chapter 5.

## Male and female love

Whether men and women are looking for the same thing when it comes to love has been the subject of considerable research. With respect to Lee's typology, there is some evidence that men are more inclined towards Ludus and Eros, while women tend more towards being storgic, pragmatic and agapic. This was the conclusion of a study by Terry Hatkoff and Thomas Lasswell based on the replies to questionnaires similar to Lee's given by 544 students and other volunteers in the south and west of the US.[12] Presumably women are inclined to be more practical about affairs of the heart because they are often economically dependent on their partners. Economic dependence was also thought to account for the fact that women in the study scored higher than men on jealousy and possessiveness – two of the main characteristics of manic love. The tendency for men to be playful and erotic is in line with their greater sexual urgency and emphasis on physical attraction and casual sex. This difference is timeless, enshrined in genes and instincts, and is discussed further in Chapter 6.

The suggestion that women are cooler in matters of the heart than men is supported by other findings. As we shall see in Chapter 2, women are less influenced by physical appearance than men and, when social lines are crossed, they are less likely to marry 'down'.[13] US sociologist William Kephart found the percentage reporting that they were 'very easily attracted to the opposite sex' was nearly twice as high for males as for females.[14]

Among his sample of over 1,000 male and female college students, Kephart found that 13 was the average age at which they had first experienced infatuation. Boys tended to be around six months behind girls. Before the age of 20 girls had more infatuations than boys. After that age, however, the number of 'romances' reported by boys continued to increase, but the girls said they had fewer. Kephart concluded that, as they mature, young women become more rational and less romantic and begin to consider the men they meet in terms of whether they would be a good, long-term prospect. Men, in contrast, are more content to pursue the romantic ideal and less concerned about the future prospects of a relationship.

In a more recent study of the love experiences of adolescents in the United States, Montgomery and Sorell found that boys fell in love earlier and more often than girls.[15] Overall, about half of those dating another person described themselves as being 'in love', with increasingly fewer people using this term to characterise their relationship as they got older. It is also interesting that twice as many men reported having loved an older woman (61 per cent) as women reported having loved a younger man (30 per cent). What's more, the women who had been romantically involved with a younger man were more likely to show evidence of maladjustment on a personality inventory and relatively poor college grades, which was not the case with men who had been involved with older women. This is not to say that there is anything necessarily abnormal about a woman falling in love with a younger man, just that in some cases it may be indicative of psychological difficulties.

Lastly, the difference between men and women is seen in their answers to the question: 'If a boy/girl had all the other qualities you desired, would you marry this person if you were not in love with him/her?' Nearly two-thirds of the boys said no, but less than one-third of the girls did so. Apart from placing less value on physical attractiveness, women seem to regard being 'in love' as less important in marital choice than do men.

## A formula for love?

American psychologist Donn Byrne has devised a formula that he claims can tell whether you are truly in love (see Figure 1.2). Based on international research over the last 20 years, Byrne concluded that the five key components of love are:

1.  sexual attraction;
2.  emotional arousal;
3.  a desire for intimacy;
4.  an intense need for the other person to want and to agree with you; and
5.  an ever-present fear of losing them.[16]

The weight to be allocated to each of these elements is, to a large extent, an individual matter and differs from one person to another. According to Byrne, sexual attraction is the most important, being necessary but not sufficient by itself. Fear of loss is the least significant factor but is nevertheless always in there somewhere. By allocating a weighting figure to each of the designated categories, and applying them in turn to a friend and to your lover, you can use the resulting totals to assess whether you are really in love with your lover. However, whatever your view of this analysis of love, if you need to do a calculation to determine whether you are in love, you probably already realise that you're not!

# The formula for love

**LOVE** = (1.7 x **A**) + (1.5 x **B**) + (1.5 x **C**) + (1.5 x **D**) + (1.3 x **E**)

**A** is sexual feelings for an average friend
**B** is the emotional arousal felt in the presence of an average friend
**C** is the desire for intimate contact with an average friend
**D** is how much you want that person to want you
**E** is the increased fear of losing that person

**How to do the calculation:**
Firstly assign a value to the strength of your friendships. This provides a standard to compare the scores for your lover.

1  Calculate the strength of your feelings for a friend on a scale of 1-10. A friend who is not missed when absent would score 5. The result is **A**

2  Estimate how mentally stimulating you find your friend to obtain. **B**. Five means you enjoy conversation without longing for it

3  Estimate your desire to be physically close to your friend to reach **C**. Five means you are on hugging terms

4  Calculate how much you care whether your friend wants your company. One means you do not care. This is **D**

5  Estimate how upset you would be if your friendship ended. Five would represent the end of a friendship with someone you liked but who had never visited your home. The result is **E**

6  Place scores of **A, B, C, D** and **E** into the equation to get **F**

7  Now repeat the same steps for your lover to reach a total, **L**

If **F** is greater than **L** you are **NOT** in love

Figure 1.2  Byrne's formula for love (from The Sunday Times, 25 April 1999)

## Love and marriage

Although some researchers have attempted to take account of the different conceptions of love prevalent at different historical periods and in different cultures, many have (perhaps inevitably) used young Americans, often their students, as the subjects of their studies. (It is important to stress that these young people are heterosexual, and mainly white.) In reality, acceptable definitions of love, especially as a basis for long-term partnership and parenthood, are not constants in terms of time or place.

Most people in modern industrialised societies take it for granted that what we call romantic love is the only basis for marriage or partnership, even if we accept that being 'in love' is only a temporary phase. Yet this kind of love has not always been the foundation upon which marriages have been built, and still isn't in some societies. Up until the end of the 19th century among the middle and upper classes in Western countries (the only groups for which much evidence exists on which to base any judgements), marriages were primarily social alliances, binding families of equal or similar status, protecting property rights and economic relations of various kinds. Even in the novels of Jane Austen, where great play is made of romance, relationships between socially ill-matched couples are discouraged and portrayed as doomed to failure. This is why Anne Elliot, heroine of *Persuasion*, is initially talked out of marrying the young Captain Wentworth – at the time he has no prospects worthy of the daughter of a baronet – and why, in *Pride and Prejudice*, Mr Darcy has to battle to overcome his family pride before he can 'descend' to marriage with Elizabeth Bennett (who has close relations who are 'in trade'). One subplot that sheds an interesting light on the tendency of women to be less romantic than men in their choice of partner is Elizabeth's disapproval of her friend Charlotte Lucas's decision to marry a man she can never love for the sake of ensuring herself a comfortable home!

That is not to say, as some psychologists, including Donn Byrne, have argued, that romantic love is a recent invention; rather that it has not always been synonymous with marriage. From earliest times, Western literature has dealt extensively with love, and modern readers have no difficulty identifying with the emotions portrayed by writers and poets down the centuries. More often than not, however, authors ranging from the Roman poet Catullus to Dante and Shakespeare were writing about what we would define as adulterous relationships, or unhappy love affairs that did not lead to marriage. In such writings, passionate or romantic love is socially disruptive, sometimes tolerated provided it is not allowed to disturb the fabric of marriage, but usually discouraged by religious and other authorities.

One of the earliest attempts to establish romantic love on a different footing was made by the knights of 12th-century France. In a recent development of his love styles paradigm, John Lee has suggested that this new 'social class' placed individual attraction above social considerations in their choice of partners for love and sex. According to him, this was the beginning of the growth of the idea of romantic love as the basis for marriage.[17]

Although they are in decline worldwide, even in societies where they were previously the norm, arranged marriages have a long history. It may go against current ideas about romantic love being the only acceptable basis for marriage, but the fact is that many of the young men and women who met for the first time at their wedding grew to love one another and remained happily together in lifelong partnerships.[18] Steve Derne notes that in a society based on extended families, such as that of high-caste urban Hindu men in north India, romantic love is regarded as a potentially dangerous – because disruptive – emotion that is therefore simultaneously undesirable and appealing.[19] Other researchers have suggested that romantic love can only be tolerated as a basis for marriage or long-term pairings when the society concerned has a measure of social equality between men and women, allowing both the freedom to choose whom to love. When women, but not men, are punished for pre- or extra-marital sex, romantic love tends not to be regarded as an acceptable foundation for marriage.

As far as Western countries are concerned, the belief that romantic love should be the precondition for marriage was gaining ground during the 19th century, but it was with the coming of the 'talking pictures' early in the last century that it started to predominate. From its earliest days, Hollywood seized on love and all its dramatic possibilities as a major theme and, although there are some exceptions, love is generally seen as all conquering. In recent times, there has been a tendency to quirky, ironic comedies of love, such as *Four Weddings and a Funeral*, *When Harry met Sally* and *Sleepless in Seattle*, but even these films conclude with the lovers finally united. The cultural clashes between the traditional and modern bases for marriage have been tackled in films such as *East is East*, where the British-born sons of a Pakistani immigrant father refuse to accept his plans for them to marry the 'suitable' young women that he has chosen for them but whom they find unattractive, to say the least. Although the script offers an insight into the logic of the father's behaviour and the inevitability of conflict when children are brought up in a different culture from their parents, the film tacitly assumes that he is unreasonable in expecting his sons to marry without love.

Despite their many and various disagreements about what constitutes love, most researchers assume it has a vital part to play in human relationships. Nevertheless, recent demographic studies have drawn attention to the increasing numbers of people in Western industrialised countries who live alone, often without any love partner on the scene. Whether this is an existence to be admired and emulated or a sad reflection of a breakdown in human relations is a matter of opinion, but the fact is that for an ever-growing proportion of these populations, the absence of a loving partner is, and for many may remain, a fact of life.

# 2

# Beauty and sex appeal

*She wore a short skirt and a tight sweater and her figure described a set of parabolas that could cause a cardiac arrest in a yak.*

Woody Allen[1]

Every relationship has to start somewhere, but we don't regard everyone of the appropriate gender whom we see or meet as a potential partner. In practice, we find ourselves strongly attracted to certain individuals, less so to others and to some not at all.

In attempting to analyse what makes someone attractive, the obvious place to begin is with the way they look, because that is usually the first thing we notice. In everyday life, we compare notes with friends and often find we disagree strongly about the desirability of particular people – whether they are individuals whom we know or see or 'fantasy' figures such as film or TV stars or pop singers. Impresarios who put together manufactured pop bands such as the Spice Girls or Steps consciously select different types of physique and perceived personalities to try to ensure that the band has the widest possible appeal to the target audience. For example, individuals may be chosen to play the role of the 'cute one', the 'sexy one', the 'funny one', and so on. Yet there is also a general consensus which accounts for the appeal of actors such as George Clooney or Leonardo DiCaprio to heterosexual women or Julia Roberts or Meg Ryan to straight men.

## Looks matter

The way we respond to images of people encountered almost exclusively on a TV or cinema screen may tell us something about what qualities of face and figure are required to meet the criteria of physical 'beauty'. This is important because there is much evidence that people who are perceived as good-looking have an advantage when it comes to succeeding in many aspects of life, including socially and at work.[2] That is not to say that good looks are the only thing that count. A person who seems attractive at a first encounter because they look good may turn out, on closer acquaintance, to have all kinds of unappealing personality traits that outweigh their physical attractiveness. It's also true that we may acknowledge that a particular individual is conventionally good-looking yet feel no spark of attraction – there is undoubtedly more to sex appeal than physical beauty. Most of us can think of at least one person among our acquaintances and friends who scores low on conventional criteria of good looks yet never lacks for lovers or admirers. As former US Secretary of State Henry Kissinger, whose best friends would not call him conventionally good-looking, once observed: 'Power is the best aphrodisiac'. Despite these genuine reservations, appearance deserves serious consideration as a factor in sexual attractiveness.

The power of good looks to convince us that a person is attractive inside is partly due to the fact that, initially, this is all we may have to go on. Having received an initial impression, probably within seconds of first seeing someone, we make up our minds that they are indeed attractive and, because we are inclined to be lazy, we may continue to act on that impression, even if closer acquaintance reveals less desirable characteristics in that individual. This kind of behaviour tends to have a snowball effect. By giving off subtle signals that we find someone appealing, we are encouraging them to respond to us in a way that reinforces that conviction. This helps to explain why good-looking people do well in most arenas of life. Other people are nice to them, show them respect and promote their wellbeing, and thus they develop greater self-confidence and self-belief, so adding positive personal qualities to their initial gift of good looks.

Evolutionary psychologists argue that, whatever our conscious minds may tell us to the contrary, we are strongly influenced by our genes when it comes to choosing a sexual partner. They take the view that reproduction is really what the mating game is about, and it makes sense in evolutionary terms to select a co-parent who is genetically equipped to ensure the birth and survival of healthy children. According to this argument, appearance is important in a potential partner because it offers clues as to whether the person is a 'good bet' from a genetic point of view.

## Women's features

For a woman to be regarded as attractive in most societies, the vital physical features are those that convey an impression of youth, because this is associated with fertility. They also tend to be signals of femininity, that is to say, attributes that differentiate the female from the male physique. Thus the 'ideal' woman has smooth skin, large, well-spaced eyes, narrow, well-defined eyebrows, plump lips, a small nose and chin and a relatively insignificant jaw, indicating that female hormones predominate over male ones. Many of these characteristics become less pronounced with increasing age – the cheekbones become more prominent and the lips less full, for example.

The way a person's facial appearance changes may also be related to their personality. Sulky children used to be told 'If the wind changes, you'll get stuck like that', meaning that the unattractive facial expression would become fixed. There is, in fact, some evidence that a person's 'resting expression' may reflect their habitual state of mind to some extent; whether happy, sad or irritable. On the other hand, a person who constantly smiles in an effort to please may trigger the so-called 'artifice effect': in other words, while their resting expression may be a vestigial smile, others recognise that it is not a true reflection of their inner self.

The situation can be further complicated by other factors. For example, while a 'babyface' may be seen as acceptable in girls or young women because it is traditionally regarded as appropriately feminine, boys and young men may try to counter the impression given by a natural babyface by becoming more aggressive and hostile, and thus more 'masculine'.[3]

From the unconscious point of view of the woman herself, a young or even childlike appearance may foster a man's nurturing instinct, encouraging him to stay with and care for her and her children. The instinct to care for the young seems to be hard-wired into the brains of adult humans. The ways in which female features differ from those of men reflect infant signals – large eyes, smooth skin and so on, the better to elicit help from males.

## Babyfaces

Much research reinforces the idea that having a babyface enhances a person's attractiveness. This has always been seen as the case with women, but a study conducted in 1999 at the University of St Andrews in Scotland suggested that the same might be true of men.[4] The researchers, led by David Perrett, working in conjunction with colleagues in Japan, used computers to alter faces so that the shape and features appeared more feminised or masculinised. When subjects in both countries were asked to rate the photos, they judged the more feminine features to be most appealing, whether they were looking at photos of men or women. This runs counter to the traditional idea that women regard 'masculine-looking' men as more attractive, on the assumption that such features imply qualities such as aggression and skill at hunting. The researchers suggest that evolution has managed to strike a balance between different desirable qualities. While it is good for a man to be strong and powerful in battle it is also important that he has an altruistic, caring side to him so that he will look after his wife and children properly.

However, it is possible that the results of Perrett and his colleagues reflect the difference between male beauty as an artistic concept (which is more 'feminine') and sex appeal (which is much more 'macho' – at least where women's preferences are concerned). The feminised faces were also judged as being younger, which might help to explain the preferences, younger people being generally regarded as more beautiful. Leonardo DiCaprio is seen as 'pretty' by young women, perhaps also by some older women who would like to 'mother' him, but the majority of mature women would probably prefer Sean Connery as a sex partner.

Men with hyper-male attributes do have an advantage when it comes to finding partners and having children. The cliché that women tend to go for the 'tall, dark and handsome' individual is apparently not far off the mark. A team of researchers in Liverpool and Poland recently analysed the medical records of a group of over 3,000 Polish men aged between 20 and 60.[5] They reported that height was a very significant factor in determining whether a man married and had children. Fathers in the group were, on average, 3 centimetres taller than men with no children. Unmarried men were also considerably shorter than married men. The only exception to this finding was in the sub-group of men who were born in the 1930s and who would, therefore, have been in the marriage market in the 1950s, a time when the losses during the Second World War would have reduced the availability of young men.

## *Hormonal factors*

The reason why men value youthful appearance in a woman is related to the fact that it is an indicator of her hormonal status and thus of her potential fertility. Two doctors – one male, one female – estimated the age of a group of women patients attending their clinic in Germany for the first time. They then measured the level of the female hormone oestrogen in the women's blood, and found that they had tended to under-estimate the age of those women with high levels, and had over-estimated that of the women with low levels. Their guesses were out by as much as eight years in some cases.[6]

## *The waist–to–hip ratio*

While her face may be childlike, the 'ideal' woman should also have pronounced adult female sexual characteristics. After puberty, the body shapes of boys and girls start to diverge under the influence of their respective sex hormones. In early adolescence, young women begin to store fat around the lower parts of their bodies, whereas young men of the same age lose fat from these areas but begin to accumulate it around their abdomens and upper bodies. A pioneering study at the University of Texas at Austin by Devendra Singh revealed that the way fat is distributed is a very significant factor when it comes to assessing female attractiveness.[7] By measuring the relative distribution of fat in these regions, researchers defined typical waist-to-hip ratios (WHRs – literally, waist size divided by hip size. Men store fat above the waist, women below). The ratio for healthy young women is between 0.67 and 0.8, whereas for men it is between 0.85 and 0.95. A low WHR is associated with desirable qualities in a woman, such as fertility, youth, high levels of female hormones and a lower level of risk for certain illnesses. Interestingly, a woman's WHR tends to increase after the menopause – when she ceases to be fertile –

as production of female hormones declines and her fat distribution becomes more like that of a man. Subjects asked to rate women using illustrations in which the WHR was varied confirmed that, provided it is not excessive, a low WHR is seen as more attractive. What is more, it mattered little whether the woman was of normal weight, underweight or overweight – as long as the WHR remained low she was seen as sexually attractive.

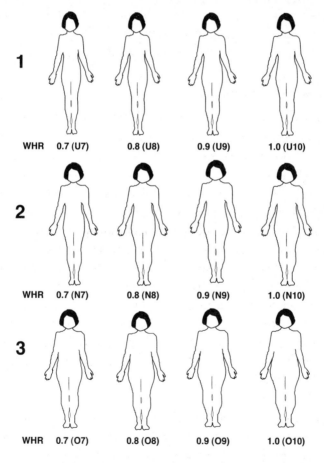

Figure 2.1  Female figures representing three body weight categories (rows) and four waist-to-hip ratios (columns) (from Singh, 1993)

Singh's studies were conducted using line drawings, but further work by psychologist Ronald Henss used three digitally modified photos of each of six women, the only difference between each set of photos being the WHR.[8] The study also controlled which aspects of the individual in the photos the subjects were asked to consider. This more subtle approach confirmed that a low WHR is widely perceived as a major factor in assessing how attractive a woman is. It is important not to push this argument to extremes: an unusually low WHR would not be rated as attractive by most subjects, and other factors, notably the face, are extremely important in judging attractiveness. Nevertheless, this work does suggest that people do subconsciously take account of a woman's fitness for reproduction, as reflected in her waist-to-hip ratio, when judging her physical attractiveness. Viewed in this light, the fabled female concern, 'Does my bum look big in this?' ought to be replaced with 'Does my WHR look high in this?'

The male equivalent of a small WHR seems to be a narrow pelvis. If women are pressed regarding the physical attributes of men they find appealing, apart from tallness, they most frequently mention a 'small, compact bottom'.[9] Presumably, they see in this an indication of testosterone and general fitness. Viewed from behind, narrow hips are the easiest way of telling a man from a woman, hence they signal masculinity.

## Hair and eye colour

Early studies that attempted to pinpoint the features considered most attractive to the opposite sex generally used white US college students as subjects and they were only asked to assess the physical characteristics of their own ethnic group. For example, one study in the late 1970s at the University of Wyoming asked students to rate factors such as eye, hair and skin colour in order of preference.[10] Results showed that in general, the common stereotype held true: men preferred light-skinned blondes with blue eyes, while women favoured dark-haired, dark-eyed men and particularly disliked light complexions and freckled skin. The authors noted the very low percentage of subjects who preferred red hair (7 per cent of male choices, 2 per cent of female).

Stereotyping obviously plays a part in the way individuals assess one another, something that most of us recognise from our own experience. There are many studies that reinforce this view; for example, researchers at Trinity College, Dublin reported that men tend to attribute a lower IQ to blonde women as compared to brunettes. Red-headed women were generally perceived to be temperamental and rather difficult.[11] Another study at the University of Northern Iowa found their subjects assessed red-headed women as unattractive but also as more competent and professional. Red-headed men fared particularly badly: their image was generally negative. Not only were they regarded as unattractive but also as less successful and more effeminate than dark or fair men.[12] Although these studies were done in the 1980s, current attitudes to 'gingers' seem to have changed little, despite the success of high-profile figures such as Chris Evans and the former Ginger Spice, Geri Halliwell.

## Symmetry

As someone, amusingly, once put it, 'The important thing about a person is that they have one of everything down the middle and two of everything down the sides'. Although mostly unaware of it at a conscious level, we are likely to find symmetry attractive in a prospective partner. This was first discovered in the 19th century by the Victorian genius Sir Francis Galton. Using the technique of composite photography, Galton found that faces that averaged the features

of people of each gender were judged to be very beautiful. This
inevitably meant that the two sides of the face were very
similar.

A Canadian study reported in 1999 confirmed the
expectation that the closer the match between the left and right
sides of the body, the more sexual success a man is likely to
have.[13] What's more, this study suggests that this desirable
symmetry is more often found in first-born sons than in their
younger brothers. According to Dr Martin Lalumière and his
associates at the Centre for Addiction and Mental Health in
Toronto, the explanation might lie in the hostile reaction of a
pregnant woman's immune system to a male foetus.
Theoretically, this potentially damaging response might
become more severe with each successive son, so while the first
boy might be relatively unaffected, his later-born brothers
would show its effects in the form of physical asymmetry.
Female foetuses would, it is suggested, be protected from this
effect by not producing testosterone to trigger the hostile
immune reaction.

Other work has shown that not only do symmetrical men
attract partners more easily, but the women concerned are
more likely to have an orgasm during sex with such a man. In
a study carried out at New Mexico University by Randy
Thornhill and colleagues, regular orgasms were found to be 40
per cent more common among the partners of men who, as a
series of measurements showed, had highly symmetrical
bodies.[14] Presumably, the increased chance of an orgasm results
from the fact that women find well-balanced, genetically
desirable men more attractive and, hence, more exciting. In a
related study, Thornhill reported that beauty and brains were
linked – at least among his research subjects. Those whose left
side closely mirrored their right scored better on IQ tests – an
indication, according to the professor, that their genetic make-
up had equipped their brains and bodies to cope optimally with

the rigours of life in the womb and the early developmental years. In other words, symmetry in both face and body is attractive because it is a sign of health and fitness.

## Fashion and culture

Some recent work has looked at the significance of fashion and the degree to which a person's attractiveness may be assessed according to ephemeral as opposed to deep-seated evolutionary criteria. For example, while women have traditionally been thought to prefer men with a full head of dark hair, a trend originally set by actors and footballers for shaven or close-cropped heads has become popular with many young, fashion-conscious men who have not yet begun to lose their hair naturally. In the last century, few men were willing to emulate icons such as the actors Yul Brynner and Sean Connery, whose lack of hair certainly did not detract from their sex appeal. On the contrary, the extreme efforts made by the likes of Frank Sinatra, Elton John and many others to restock their thinning hair were well publicised and imitated by those who could afford to do so. Flowing locks have been regarded in the past as a symbol of male sexual potency and their loss an indication of decline – the archetype perhaps being the Biblical story of Samson, whose power was destroyed when Delilah cut off his hair. However, baldness is a two-edged signal, indicating both testosterone and age, so there is room for cultural variability.

The image of what constitutes the desirable female form might also appear to be changing – if we were to judge purely on the basis of those women who feature most prominently in newspapers and magazines and on cinema and TV screens. Few women in Western society today would aspire to the rounded voluptuousness of classical sculpted figures such as the Venus de Milo or the women painted by Rubens. Most aspire rather to imitate the slim – some would say unhealthily thin – figures of popular actresses and supermodels, such as Calista Flockhart and Kate Moss.

Definitions of beauty are always culturally influenced. Although Westernised images of ultra-thin women may be having some effect on perceptions of what constitutes the ideal as far as women are concerned, in many non-Western countries such relative emaciation is still not regarded as attractive or desirable by either sex. US psychologist Nancy Etcoff has argued that an individual's concept of what constitutes beauty is at least partly determined by experience.[15] Thus, as the Western media increasingly features images of well-known actors and models from minority ethnic groups, their physical traits – such as Asian or African features, body shapes and hair and skin colours – are being partially incorporated into a wider view of the ideal. At the same time, in countries like India and the West Indies, lighter skin tones are valued, perhaps because of the pervasiveness of white Western culture and images.

Despite these apparent fluctuations, many psychologists would argue that the fundamentals imposed by evolution are basically unchanged. Most modern heterosexual men still prefer voluptuous women, as typified by *Penthouse* centrefolds, and generally do not find the skinny women on the catwalk desirable; fashion designers select models whose figures make them effective clothes horses and whose curves will not compete for attention with the designs they are showing off. In addition, fashion, by definition, depends upon change to differentiate itself from whatever came previously. It is often, therefore, totally opposed to the ideals of classical beauty and ignores sex appeal (as defined by evolutionary fitness) altogether.

The reproductive imperative remains vitally important when choosing a partner because the drive to produce and rear healthy offspring is the prime concern – however much sophisticated modern men and women may have lost sight of this fact on a conscious level. From a broader perspective, evolution is also said to explain why men and women tend to have different perspectives on personal relationships. From a man's point of view, the prime objective is to spread his sperm as widely as possible so as to optimise the chances of his genes being passed on to the maximum number of offspring. Conversely, a woman has fewer opportunities to pass on her genes, and her biological aim must therefore be to select a 'good quality' partner who will stay around and help to provide materially for her and her child. Thus the criteria used by men and women to select a partner will be different, and this inevitably implies some level of inbuilt conflict of interest, which must be resolved if both parties' interests are to be served.

## In the heat of the moment

Whether your taste runs to fair hair or dark, skinny or shapely, it seems that your emotional state when you encounter an attractive person may influence your response to them. One significant experiment by researchers at the University of Vancouver involved two groups of men walking across bridges: one an ordinary, undramatic one and the other a suspension bridge with low handrails that swayed alarmingly above a 230-foot drop. As they reached the other side, the two groups were approached by an attractive woman researcher and asked to complete a questionnaire. She also gave them her phone number and told them to ring if they wanted to discuss the experiment. The men who had crossed the suspension bridge not only included more sexual content in their replies to the questionnaire than those who had crossed the safe bridge, but significantly more of them attempted to 'chat her up' later.[16]

Apparently fear is conducive to sexual attraction and love, a principle that has led certain British theme parks to offer singles' nights described as 'adrenaline dates'. The above and

other related studies led to the formation of a theory as to why
emotional arousal should predispose people to think they are in
love. It seems that the experience of any given emotion
involves two separate stages. The first is an awareness of
physiological arousal (such as fast breathing, rapid heartbeat);
the second is labelling that arousal as a particular emotion, such
as anger, fear or love. The rules for this labelling are learned
from other people, both directly and through the mass media,
and a person will experience love only if they conclude that
love is an appropriate label for their feelings of arousal. If you
are being thrown about on a white-knuckle ride with an
attractive person you are likely to conclude that you must be in
love with them.

Support for this 'attribution theory', as it is called, comes from
experiments in which subjects are injected with adrenaline (a
drug that produces a general arousal reaction). The emotional
experience that they describe is found to depend on their
cognitive appraisal of the situation; for example, what effect they
expect the drug to have and the way in which other people
supposedly on the drug are seen to behave.

Sexual arousal would seem particularly well placed to be
labelled (or mislabelled) as love, which might explain why both
sexual gratification and frustration have been cited by different
theorists as conducive to romantic love. What at first sight
seems like a contradiction is easily accounted for by attribution
theory. A person who is aroused in the presence of an attractive
partner either because sexual consummation is blocked or
because gratification has been achieved may, under appropriate
circumstances, classify their emotion as love. Stuart Valins has
shown that even the erroneous belief that a woman has excited
a man can facilitate his attraction to her.[17] Male college students
were given false feedback concerning their heart rate as they
looked at a series of *Playboy* pin-ups. For some of the slides they
were told that their heartbeat had quickened, while for others

there was no reaction. When the men were subsequently asked to rate the women in the pictures, they preferred the ones they thought had aroused them. They preferred the same women even when they were interviewed again a month later in a totally different context.

Other experiments support the idea that a person's sexual attractiveness is influenced by the arousal of the other. In one study, male subjects first ran on the spot to increase their physical arousal. After a brief rest they were shown videos of a woman. Some saw her attractively dressed and made-up and sounding lively; the others saw her looking drab and sounding dull. The results showed that the highly aroused men found the 'attractive' woman more appealing and the 'unattractive' woman less so than did an unaroused control group.

In a second experiment, subjects heard one of three tapes. The first was grisly news footage, the second comedy and the third an extract from a biology textbook. These were classified by the researchers as negative, positive and neutral, respectively. Both the positive and negative tapes, which stimulated arousal, had the same effect on attractiveness ratings as did the jogging session.[18]

Since physical arousal seems to be connected to the way we respond to an attractive person, it is interesting to consider whether we might be able to control this response and whether it would make any difference if we were aware that we were aroused. Craig Foster and colleagues had 40 students exercise for a period of several minutes. They were then shown photos of women and asked to say how attractive they found them. Half of the men were asked to remember a seven-digit number while they were giving their assessment. Those given the mental task rated the women more highly than those who had not been similarly distracted. The authors suggest that we know our own physical arousal makes a person seem more attractive than they really are and can compensate for this when making a judgement, unless our brain is preoccupied with some other mental activity.[19]

## 'The parent trap'

At various times, psychologists have suggested that individuals will be sexually attracted to people who resemble the parent of the opposite sex. In other words, a boy will tend to fall in love with a girl who shares certain of his mother's physical characteristics, while a girl will prefer a boy who reminds her in some way of her father. The classic version of this analysis was Sigmund Freud's concept of the Oedipus complex, which was central to his psychoanalytic theory. Little boys, thought Freud, went through a phase of sexually desiring their mothers and fearing castration by their jealous fathers. While few men today are likely to acknowledge this as a factor in defining their own sexual preferences, could the theory nevertheless contain an element of truth?

Anecdotal support for Oedipal attraction is plentiful. For example, a 43-year-old woman was convicted of incest in a court in Tennessee because she had unwittingly married the son whom she had given up for adoption shortly after he was born. Instances of compelling attraction between siblings are common. Kim Straker and Terri Bigham were ordered to live apart by a judge in Essex because, despite being brother and sister, they had had a child together. They had met in 1985 after being adopted and separated for 25 years after their parents had died, and fell instantly in love. 'It was like a lightning bolt the first time I looked at Terri,' said Kim. Although cast out by the law and by their own families, they vowed to carry on loving one another, even if it meant being sent to prison.[20]

The increasing frequency with which adopted individuals have been able to make contact again with long-lost relatives has resulted in many reports of striking and immediate sexual attraction between genetically close people.[21] However, as with the original characters in the Greek myth, Oedipus and his mother/wife Jocasta, early separation seems to be a vital factor. Research in animals shows that they are loath to copulate with those with whom they have been reared and studies of the Israeli kibbutzim show that incest avoidance goes beyond biological siblings, extending to all those in the same family unit. Apparently, where sexual desire is concerned, familiarity breeds contempt.

If family similarity is sexually attractive in the absence of over-exposure, what could be the source of this attraction? A likely candidate is early childhood imprinting. In many instances, the brain of an animal is primed genetically to search for a particular stimulus configuration in the environment, consolidating the detail according to what is actually available. Thus the first moving object that resembles the mother goose will be followed relentlessly by the goslings. Sexual targets are imprinted in a similar way, such that a baboon isolated from other members of its species may become sexually fixated on something inappropriate, like the gumboots of its keeper. Likewise, many a dog owner has been embarrassed by the fact that their pet may be just as aroused by human visitors as by another dog. Since they are raised by human beings, dogs' sexual desires often follow suit.

The opposite sex parent seems to be a powerful model for the imprinting of sexual targets. If a Japanese quail is raised by an albino mother it is likely to be turned on by albino mates in adulthood. The same applies to mammals. Dr Keith Kendrick and his team at Cambridge took 13 sheep and eight goats from their natural mothers soon after birth and gave them to mothers of the other species to be reared.[22] It is known that, like humans, nanny goats and ewes bond strongly with their offspring and, in this experiment, the foster mothers bonded effectively with their 'adopted' charges. The lambs and kids behaved as though they were in fact members of their adopted mothers' species, and once adult, attempted to mate with members of that species rather than their own. Interestingly, male animals tended to take on their new species identity more firmly than females. They were apparently less adaptable than the females, who reverted more easily to their natural species behaviour when given sufficient contact with animals of their own kind. A possible explanation for this difference is that male animals are more dependent on imprinting processes to establish their sexual targets. Particular sights and smells become linked to sexual excitement in an inflexible, fetishistic kind of way, comprising cues that promote a 'promiscuity strategy'. Females tend to be more responsive than predatory in their sexual behaviour and perhaps react to pheromones produced by males of their own species.

Human studies confirm the existence of an Oedipal component in mate selection. Hawaii is an ethnic melting pot, with roughly even numbers of Polynesian, Oriental and European people, who frequently intermarry. Research shows that where a child has parents of different races, he or she is inclined to marry into the ethnic group to which the opposite sex parent belongs. In other words, boys use their mother as a sexual blueprint and girls use their father. This principle has been confirmed in Britain with respect to eye colour, with girls tending to fall in love with boys whose eye colour matches that of their father rather than their mother. It also applies to age, in that a girl whose father was middle-aged when she was born is more likely to be attracted to older men when she grows up.[23]

Of course, each of these effects is slight and must be measured statistically, because there are many aspects of our opposite sex parent that we might be seeking to replicate in a sexual partner. It is also important to remember that our blueprint for arousal is based on our parents as they were in our childhood, not as they are when we are adults. This would explain why many middle-aged men are turned on by stockings and suspenders; modern women rarely wear them but the men's mothers probably did when they were infants.

The problem from an evolutionary point of view is that using parents as a sexual blueprint could result in harmful inbreeding. Since most individuals carry 20 or 30 genes that could cause serious hereditary disease, the risk of a miscarriage or the birth of a child with disabilities is increased when close relatives mate. This is the natural logic underlying the abhorrence of incest and, although the familiarity factor is often sufficient to prevent it occurring, it is also possible that we are born with mechanisms that lead us to choose a partner who differs from our parents and siblings. Research by Patrick Bateson at Cambridge University shows that some animals prefer to mate with an unfamiliar cousin rather than an unfamiliar sibling or an unrelated individual.[24] This suggests that attraction is based on the recognition of genetic similarity while being controlled by another instinct pushing us towards optimal out-breeding. Thus we may actually be seeking a balance between the familiar and the exotic.

# 3

# Take your partners

*I married beneath me. All women do.*

Nancy Astor

As we have seen, when two people first meet and are attracted to one another sexually, they are likely to be responding in large part to visible physical attributes. Of course, some individuals are more body conscious than others; they're put off by someone they see as too short, too fat or even by something like red hair, while others are less influenced by looks. Nevertheless, physical attraction can only take you so far. What if the person turns out on closer acquaintance to have unattractive personality traits or you simply find them impossible to get on with? What determines whether you will find them to be on your wavelength, prefer their company to that of other possible partners, and want to have a loving relationship with them?

Not all promising encounters develop into an actual relationship. In the early stages, either or both people may employ a range of strategies and tactics designed to draw the interest of their target and there is plenty of scope for things to go awry. In some instances, it may never go beyond flirtation, perhaps because one person is not sufficiently interested in getting more involved or because they simply enjoy the thrill of the chase and are not really interested in anything beyond that. Even if one person is hoping to find the love of their life or is at least looking for a committed relationship, the other may only want a casual affair. With so many possible variations inherent in any initial encounter, it is indicative of the human desire to establish loving relationships that so many people do manage to navigate all the obstacles and actually 'take their partners'.

## Making the play

From the moment you set eyes on another person, you are making unconscious assessments of them based on their appearance. All of us do this all the time, whether we're sitting on a train, watching TV or meeting strangers at a party. To a large extent, these initial judgements are based on mental stereotypes – what we think the person's clothes, hairstyle and so on tell us about the type of person they are. For example, women who wear glasses are often seen as more serious or intelligent than those who do not; men with a skinhead may be perceived as threatening. Of course, if you meet and get to know someone, the reality of their personality may be superimposed onto the initial assessments and even change them completely, but if you find a person unattractive because of some aspect of the way they present themselves, you will probably not make an effort to find out whether they are not as they appear to be.

It is often said that when having a conversation, around two-thirds of what you take in about another person (and what they take in about you) is conveyed not in actual words but through visual signals: the way they stand or sit, their facial expressions, movements, proximity and so on. Although it is possible to analyse this body language and ascribe specific meanings to it few people are aware of it on a conscious level, nor are they able to manipulate their own non-verbal signals consistently and convincingly. For example, a man and a woman who are attracted to one another will tend to make frequent eye contact and hold one another's gaze. They stand or sit with their muscles tightened, and 'point' their bodies towards each other, in such a way as to discourage other people from joining their tête-à-tête. They will smile frequently, reduce the amount of physical space between them and may touch one another in seemingly casual or accidental ways. Such gestures and postures are interpreted positively, although some people are more responsive to them than others, but almost everyone can recognise the signals that convey lack of interest: yawning, frowning, looking around the room or moving away from the other person.

Some non-verbal cues are even less apparent but nevertheless have a powerful impact. One experimenter showed men two photos of the same woman, identical in every respect except that in one her pupils had been touched up to make them appear larger.[1] Most people picked the photo with the enlarged pupils as being the more attractive, even though they were frequently unable to spot the difference between the two. It is known that our pupils dilate when we are aroused and interested in what we are looking at. Apparently this may be transmitted as a sexual signal without our being aware of it. Women in medieval Italy were, however, well aware of this phenomenon and would put drops of belladonna into their eyes to make their pupils larger – it's no coincidence that *bella donna* actually means beautiful woman! Maybe this is what we are referring to when we say that someone has 'bedroom eyes'.

If you were to watch a couple who were getting on well together, you would probably be able to see that their body language was reflecting the level of communication between them. For example, they would tend to adopt parallel physical postures – crossing and uncrossing the opposite leg, moving their arms and hands in synch and making similar gestures. This is known variously as mirroring, synchrony or postural echo and can be observed in any two people who are on the same wavelength – friends as well as lovers and would-be lovers.

The reason why this kind of communication is so important is that it indicates that our interest in the other person is reciprocated, and most of us have a natural tendency to be attracted to people who show that they feel the same way about us. However, various studies have shown that things are not always quite that simple. There is evidence to show that we respond even more positively to people who initially seem relatively uninterested or even hostile but then appear to change their minds.

## Playing hard to get

One of the earliest studies on the effectiveness of blowing cold then hot was conducted by Aronson and Linder.[2] Their subjects had a conversation with a person briefed by the researchers and then 'accidentally' heard this person making remarks about them to someone else. When later asked how they felt about the person they had talked to on the basis of their earlier conversation, they liked them better if the remarks they had overheard were uniformly complimentary, and tended to dislike them if their comments had been entirely derogatory. But they liked best of all those whose comments had progressed from unfavourable to favourable during the course of the experiment. This would suggest that the way to win new friends and lovers is to start by showing dislike (without being too insulting) and then show progressive interest and approval.

There are various interpretations of this 'gain phenomenon', as it has been called. One is that early disdain makes it less likely that later warmth will be perceived as habitual or ingratiating. Another explanation is in terms of self-esteem. Studies show that people who have a low opinion of themselves are less demanding in their expectations of others, including opposite sex partners. Women whose self-esteem has been lowered by rude, offhand treatment at the outset of an experiment find a man presented by the researchers more attractive than women whose self-esteem has been raised, and men who are low in self-esteem are less likely to ask an attractive woman out than men who are apparently high in self-esteem. If being rude or indifferent to somebody on first acquaintance lowers their self-esteem even temporarily, they might be more vulnerable to whatever charm we later direct towards them.

Experiments have been carried out to see whether men and women who play hard to get are perceived as more desirable. A research team had male subjects telephone a woman with whom they had supposedly been matched by computer, to arrange a meeting.[3] In fact, it was always the same woman at the other end of the phone, a confederate of the researchers. For half the men she was very available, being delighted to receive their call and grateful to be asked out; for the others she agreed to meet for coffee with some reluctance because she had many other dates and was not sure she wanted to get involved with anyone new. After this conversation, the man's impression of the woman was assessed. Results of this and similar experiments failed to support the 'hard to get' hypothesis, as the men considered the 'two women' equally desirable.

The researchers then revised their hypothesis. Perhaps the most desirable person is the one who is apparently very keen on you (that is, easy for you to get) but hard to get for everyone else. To test this 'selective difficulty' hypothesis, they used another computer date design. One woman appeared generally easy to get, making it clear she was keen to meet anyone assigned to her by the computer. Another made it clear that she was generally hard to get and not particularly eager to date any of the men assigned to her by the computer. A third woman was selective, that is, apparently eager to date the subject but not interested in any of his rivals. This time the hypothesis was vindicated: the selective woman was decisively preferred over either of the others.

One possible explanation of why playing hard to get may be effective in some situations is that the harder you have to work to gain something, the more you appreciate it when you do succeed. Several studies have demonstrated this phenomenon in different contexts. For example, applicants to join a study course were divided into two groups. The first was made to go through a rigorous selection process while the second was simply given basic information about the course, for which both groups were subsequently accepted. Follow-up showed that the first group felt they had enjoyed the course more than the second. One is reminded of Groucho Marx's comment that he would 'never want to join a club that would accept me as a member'. Perhaps the same principle applies in the fields of dating and mating.

## For ever or not?

It is widely acknowledged that, as a generalisation, men are more interested in sex while women focus on love. Back in 1975, one study tested this hypothesis in an unusually direct way. Subjects were approached with a direct proposition – they were told that the person, who was of the opposite sex, had noticed them, found them attractive and would like to have sex with them.[4] All of the women approached in this way refused; some were offended, some insulted and some simply puzzled. The men, on the other hand, were far more likely to be flattered and agree to the suggestion – 75 per cent did so when approached. Of those who refused, many took the trouble to apologise and explain why they had to say no, often explaining that they already had a regular partner. If such an experiment were to be repeated today, it would probably get much the same result; even if a few women might possibly react differently, it is highly unlikely that the majority would.

Nevertheless, simple logic implies that, if men are to put their desire for multiple partners into practice, there must be at least some women who are willing to have a sexual relationship without any long-term commitment on the man's part. Women are more variable than men with respect to indulgence in casual sex. From the many studies, ranging from the ground-breaking ones conducted by Kinsey in the middle of the 20th century, through later scientific studies and the informal surveys of Shere Hite and others, it is clear that the average man is more inclined to have multiple sexual liaisons than the average woman. David Buss and colleagues found that women who did go in for what he calls 'short-term mating' perceived the benefits and possible costs of such relationships differently to those women who did not.[5] The benefits perceived by the women who did pursue short-term mating were increased sexual variety and pleasure, increasing their ability to attract men, material gains — such as expensive clothes — and practical gains such as career advancement. They were also less concerned that having a variety of partners would damage their reputation and status. The study found that such women often cited problems with their long-term partner as the reason why they sought out alternatives.

Differences in the way people see themselves in terms of their value in what might be called the 'sexual market-place' appeared to influence whether they were interested in casual sexual relationships, according to the findings of one study conducted in 1995.[6] Men who regarded themselves as 'high value' started having sex at a younger age and had sex more often with a greater variety of women throughout their lives. The same was not true of women who rated themselves as 'high value'. What did seem to be significant as far as women were concerned was their level of self-esteem: those with low self-esteem reported having had more partners, including more one-night stands, and had a preference for brief relationships.

Again, men differed in that their self-esteem did not appear to be related to a history of early sex or multiple, short-term partners.

## 'What you really, really want…'

If asked, most people could come up with a list of attributes that they would like their ideal partner to possess, even though they are probably realistic enough to know that one person is unlikely to have them all. Some attempts have been made to find out not only what qualities are most sought after, but also which ones generate the most response from potential partners, by analysing the content of and responses to lonely hearts advertisements. In 1995, Baize and Schroeder looked at 195 such ads placed in two different US newspapers.[7] They contacted the advertisers and asked them to complete a questionnaire about the number and type of people who had replied to their ads. They then compared these to the information included in the advertisers' self-descriptions. The results showed that women were more likely to respond to men who were older, who mentioned or hinted that they earned a good salary and who were well educated. The authors summed up their findings with a neat reference to the question asked by singer/songwriter Tim Hardin in his 1960s song: 'If I were a carpenter and you were a lady, would you marry me anyway?' Apparently not, concluded Baize and Schroeder.

Among other interesting findings in this study was the fact that more men replied to such ads than women; the men received about two-thirds the number of letters that women received. Predictably, women who referred to themselves as 'physically attractive' got a bigger response than those who didn't. Although women were also more likely to write to the men who claimed to be attractive, the effect of this claim was less striking as far as male advertisers were concerned.

Mentioning in their ads that they were 'sexually attractive' also enhanced the response that women received, but men who included this in their ads actually got fewer responses. Unsurprisingly, perhaps, younger women got more replies than older women, which suggests that the traditional pattern of men preferring younger (and thus more fertile) women still holds true.

A similar – though not identical – picture of those placing personal ads in a newspaper in a south-eastern US city was reported in 1998 by Larry Lance.[8] His analysis of 489 such ads showed that, when describing themselves, both men and women emphasised personality, good looks, a professional/college degree, slimness and non-smoking. In addition, the women also mentioned their height. Ads in other publications were roughly similar, although some women specified that men must like children and have an element of what they called 'spirituality'. The earning power of the men does not feature specifically in Lance's list, although it may be inferred that this would be above average in most cases in view of their emphasis on further education. The fact that women also emphasised their level of education was taken by the author to suggest that the criteria employed by the two sexes when selecting a partner may be changing. However, it might just have been the women's way of attracting men of superior education – and hopefully intelligence and earning power.

Other studies have shown that, whenever possible, both men and women put most of the preferences specified in these ads into practice when selecting a partner. Marriage statistics collected by David Buss from 27 countries showed that, on average, the men were around three years older than their brides.[9] Many researchers have found positive correlations between the perceived attractiveness of a woman and her husband's high status and income. Such work lends support to the theory that youth and good looks are what men seek in a woman, while a man's ability to be a good provider is a more important criterion for women, whatever each may say (or even believe) to the contrary. A 1994 survey of Canadian statistics on the age differences between 6 million married and divorcing couples in Canada provides an amusingly concise guideline as to the ideal age gap. According to the statisticians' analysis, a woman who marries a man six years older than herself is the least likely to get divorced, with the single exception of one who marries a man more than 50 years her senior. He is, of course, more likely to die than divorce her!

## The 'Romeo and Juliet effect'

Once a couple have negotiated the initial stages of attraction and established that not only is it reciprocal but that there is more to their interest in each other than a passing fancy, they can begin to enter one another's world. Usually this will mean meeting friends and, often, families too, which is where things can sometimes begin to get rocky. Most parents have high aspirations for their offspring and are anxious that they should choose a partner whom they deem acceptable, whatever criteria they personally apply to this judgement. It is common for parents to disapprove of some boyfriends or girlfriends, but if they take seriously against a chosen partner, expressing their objections may be counter-productive.

An influential study conducted in 1972 by Richard Driscoll and colleagues in Colorado assessed the impact of attempts by parents to interfere in relationships of which they disapproved.[10] They asked 91 married couples and 49 unmarried pairs of lovers to complete questionnaires to measure their degree of romantic love, trust and companionship and to assess the amount of interference they had encountered in the course of their relationships. The married couples' feelings for one another seemed to have been relatively uninfluenced by their parents' reactions but the unmarried lovers seemed to become more intensely 'in love' as the level of parental interference rose. When the researchers went back to the same couples some months after the original work was done, they found that the more the parents had interfered in the meantime, the greater the passionate commitment of the couples to one another. That hurdles may strengthen romantic ties is supported by a study of couples where the two individuals were of different religions – those couples that belonged to different faiths had higher love scores than those of the same religion.[11]

There are two possible theories as to why this Romeo and Juliet effect might occur. One idea is that frustration is a significant cause of arousal, and that this in itself is sufficient to raise the level of romantic attraction. The other possible explanation is a theory known as 'cognitive dissonance', which reasons as follows: 'Everything and everybody has conspired against us and yet we are still together, therefore we must be very much in love'. The effect may appear strong partly because some weaker relationships actually break up in response to parental pressure while only the deeper, more intense relationships survive. This would also make for a correlation between parental opposition and love scores in couples who stay together despite all.

## A good match?

The cliché that opposites attract is often held to be true when it comes to loving relationships. While most people could point to examples where this does seem to apply among people they know, the weight of research evidence does not support the idea that relationships based on difference are the most successful. In fact, the equally well-known proverb 'birds of a feather flock together' seems to be a more reliable guide to relationship success. Psychologists call the birds of a feather and opposites attract approaches the 'similarity' and 'complementation' theories of attraction respectively. One of the earliest studies to back similarity theory was conducted by Donn Byrne and colleagues using American university students.[12] Once the students had completed an attitude and personality questionnaire, they were sent on a blind date – half with people similar to themselves and half with people very different. When interviewed afterwards, the students said that those partners they found most desirable were those most similar to themselves and those previously rated by the researchers as attractive.

Other researchers have found very little evidence to support the complementation theory but a great deal of similarity between partners, particularly as regards age, race, religion, social class, intelligence, political attitudes, physical attractiveness, hobbies and interests. The similarity effect is less striking with regard to personality traits but it remains a more important principle of attraction than complementation. Even the personality dimensions that would have been thought most likely to accord with the complementation principle, such as dominance and submission, show a pattern of likeness rather than opposites.

In a fairly typical study of this kind, David Nias studied the correlations between husbands and wives on various questionnaires concerning personality and interests.[13] Some of the items on which the couples were most similar are shown below (the higher the figure in brackets, the closer the correlation; if complementation had applied, the figures would be negative).

*Personality*:
Have you had more trouble than most? (.25)
Are there people who would wish to harm you? (.26)
Would you take drugs that may have strange or harmful effects?

(.21)
Are you usually very unlucky? (.29)
Do people tell you a lot of lies? (.19)
Do you like going out a lot? (.20)
Do you prefer to have few but special friends? (.19)

*Leisure*:
Going out for a drink (.34)
Going to dances (.34)
Television:
    Variety shows (.29)
    Pop music programmes (.37)

*Reading*:
Pop music magazines (.31)
Romance magazines (.22)

*Sport*:
Watching favourite sport (.40)
Watching with children (.47)

*Encouraging children*:
Music (.57)
Part-time jobs (.51)

There were a number of areas in which the couples showed no similarity at all (for example, cooking, overall time spent reading, overall amount of time spent watching adventure films and so on) but no instances in which the couples could be said to be opposite in temperament or inclination.

Other psychologists who have looked at the significance of personality in determining choice of partner have found that people generally look for similarity (known as 'assortative mating'). A study that asked people to describe their ideal partner, conducted in 1997 by Michael Botwin and colleagues, found an average correlation between the subject's own personality and that of their ideal of around .30.[14] It confirmed earlier findings that this held true even for traits such as dominance and submissiveness: dominant people wanted dominant partners and vice versa. The same appears to apply, although to a lesser degree, to introversion versus extraversion: a 1996 study found a correlation of .20 for this trait. Shared attitudes to big issues seem to be important too. Other studies have found a large measure of agreement between couples on politics and controversial areas such as capital punishment and abortion. Apart from anything else, this suggests that anyone seeking a partner through lonely hearts ads would be well advised to respond to those in newspapers that share their personal perspective on such matters: in the UK, *Guardian* readers may be less likely to find a compatible person advertising in the *Telegraph*, for example!

It might seem strange that a dominant person would seek a dominant partner since this would mean that their dominance could be asserted only outside the relationship. However, there is one sense in which complementation does apply. Where there is an average difference between men and women on an attribute (any physical or psychological trait), then a particular relationship that echoes this difference is the most stable.[15] For example, men are on average taller than women by around 5 inches, so tall men seek women who are tall, but not as tall as themselves. Similarly, short people seek a short partner, but still with the man taller than the woman. In the field of personality, men have higher dominance scores than women, while women score higher on emotionality. These personality differences tend to be reflected in partnerships such that they last better if the male partner is on the 'masculine' side of the woman but not to an excessive degree. Hence dominant men want a woman who is dominant in relation to other women but not dominant over themselves. Women, it seems, are also happiest with this arrangement; that is, however dominant they themselves are, they are still most content with a man who is more dominant.

Further evidence to support similarity theory was adduced in a study in 1972 by Richard Centers, which set out to test the theory, put forward by Freud and later writers, that people tend to fall in love with someone because they have desirable qualities that the individual perceives him- or herself as lacking.[16] This is known as 'completion theory'. For example, someone who feels shy and inept in social situations might seek a confident and socially adept partner. Centers asked 50 engaged student couples to complete questionnaires to rate themselves and their partners in terms of a range of attributes and abilities and to rate the desirability of these factors for men and for women. The results showed that most of the subjects had become engaged to someone whom they considered to be comparable to themselves in terms of social ability and entertaining ability. The same was largely true in respect of the other attributes and abilities. The author concludes that, while the completion theory might correctly describe what people might wish to do in an ideal world, it takes no account of a reality in which competition for those who are ranked high on the 'attributes and abilities' scales is intense. In other words, the shy and awkward person is unlikely to win the love of a popular, socially skilled person unless they are fortunate or have some other valued quality to offer in compensation. Therefore, they usually end up having to settle for somebody similar to themselves.

So far we have considered the relevance of similarity in terms of personality traits, attitudes and interests in general, but a slightly different light was shed on the topic by a project conducted by Jennifer Hahn and Thomas Blass.[17] Taking John Lee's six primary love styles as their starting point, they first asked 152 students, ranging in age from 18 to 41, to complete a questionnaire to indicate their own preferred love style. They were then asked to indicate which of the six people, presented to them in the form of transcribed 'interviews', they found most appealing. Each interview was designed to reflect a different love style. The results showed that, in general, the subjects were most drawn to the person whose preferred love style was closest to their own – further evidence that similarity is a prime criterion in selecting a partner. Interestingly, the most popular styles were Storge and Agape, with relatively few favouring Ludus.

In reality, couples may overestimate just how similar they are to one another, according to the findings of a study conducted by Del Thiessen and others in 1997.[18] They first asked 59 couples to rate themselves on a range of physical and psychological characteristics such as hair and eye colour, attractiveness, race, humour and interest in sex and then to make the same assessments of their partners. Although the results showed that couples resembled one another more than would have been predicted by chance, the second part of the rating assessment showed that couples actually perceived themselves as being very similar. The authors suggest two possible explanations for this: either the subjects' self-evaluations were not particularly accurate or they believed themselves to be more like their partners than they really were. Interestingly, the traits that couples were most likely to believe they shared with their partners related to their levels of interest in sex, marriage and having children. Twelve of the couples were then photographed separately, and 50 students were asked to match them into couples. They actually managed to match the right pairs three times more often than might have been expected by chance, and those who got the correct matches appeared to use cues that related to general body features, facial traits and ethnicity.

# 'Change the name and not the letter...'

'Change for worse and not for better' goes the old saying. This may have less significance today when many women choose not to adopt their husbands' surnames on marriage, but names may still be more important in determining the choice of partner than might be thought, according to a study by Richard Kopelman and Dorothy Lang.[19] The authors analysed the first names of husbands and wives collected from a variety of sources to discover how frequently couples shared first names or nicknames starting with the same initial. The frequency with which alliteration occurred varied according to the data sources used to retrieve couples' names, but nevertheless when all the samples were weighted equally, the likelihood of couples having alliterative first names was 8.3 per cent greater than would be predicted by chance and 12 per cent greater for nicknames. The authors counsel caution in interpreting these findings – the size of data sets used varied; no allowance was made for names that do not begin with the same letter but sound as if they do (for example, Susan and Cecil); less common nicknames were not included and no allowance was made for the influence of ethnicity. They also point out that results showed alliteration to have been more common in earlier generations when, to paraphrase the subtitle of their paper, Barbara was more likely to marry Barry!

If true, there are several possible interpretations. One is that people pair off partly because their names have a nice poetic ring when put together, making them sound like an item. Another is that people may be narcissistic in their choice of partner, picking someone who not only looks like themselves but also has a name that sounds like their own.

## Genetic similarity theory

A controversial approach that attempts to account for assortative mating (and other types of human and animal relationships) is 'genetic similarity theory' (GST). Its proponents suggest that GST explains the findings from many studies that partners tend to resemble one another across a wide range of characteristics – from physical attractiveness, IQ, education and attitudes to personality traits and values. In several papers published in the 1980s, J Philippe Rushton and his colleagues argue that many kinds of creatures, including humans, are able to recognise others who are genetically similar to themselves, and show a preference for such individuals when choosing sexual partners. By behaving in this way, they argue, animals maximise the chances of their genes being passed on to their offspring and subsequent generations. To support their theory, the authors point to studies showing, for example, that the more genetically similar a couple are, the more fertile they appear to be. Just how people go about recognising others with similar genetic inheritance is a matter of dispute, but it is likely to be due in part to inherited brain structures that make a particular individual seem attractive or otherwise. Other traits that seem to play an important part in assortative mating, such as intelligence, values and socio-economic status, also have a genetic component – which may be as high as 50 per cent or more. The greater the genetic weighting of such characteristics, the more significant they appear to be in terms of partner choice.[20]

One study that questions the role of genetics in mate selection was carried out by David Lykken in 1993.[21] He reasoned that if a choice of mate was determined partly by genetic factors then identical twins would pick partners that were more like one another than would fraternal twins (who are less genetically similar). In fact, with a sample of 738 middle-aged couples, he was not able to find any difference between the two twin types in this respect, leading him to conclude that mate choice 'depends on where you are when Cupid's arrow strikes'. It does, however, remain a possibility that

Cupid's arrow is forged mainly in early childhood through some process of imprinting.

## Assessing compatibility

By summing the degree of similarity between two partners across various domains that are known to be relevant to compatibility it is possible to arrive at a Compatibility Quotient (CQ) that gives an indication of how well a couple will rub together. One of the most widely used is the Wilson Compatibility Indicator (shown on pages 58–59). This was initially developed as a computer program that was used both as a research instrument and as a kind of electronic 'spin the bottle' for use at dinner parties. The simplified hand-scoring version given below was developed by an Australian psychologist called Geoffrey Dean who experimented with having advertisers in a newspaper singles' column incorporate their responses to the questionnaire in their ad as a kind of 'postcode' that would enable others to pre-assess their suitability as potential partners. It will be seen that the items cover all the areas that are known from past research to be important sources of discontent or dispute:

1. Physical traits such as height, build and attractiveness.
2. Sexual appetite and attitudes.
3. Intelligence, education and occupational type.
4. Personality, religion and politics.
5. Habits like smoking and drinking.
6. Preferences in matters such as music, entertainment and food.

Each item forms a scale, such that the further away from each other the responses of the two individuals the less likely they are to hit it off together. If the total of all discrepancies is very high the couple are unlikely to form a lasting, satisfying relationship. Of course, similarity in such arenas is not the only thing that determines whether a couple will be attracted to each other. The chemistry, to be discussed next, is also important. What the CQ tells you is whether your long-term prospects are good after the early passion has cooled.

Table 3.1 Wilson Compatibility Indicator

This questionnaire can be used to calculate the degree of compatibility (suitability for a long-term relationship) between any pair of people. Follow these steps:

1. Each partner completes the form (separately without consultation)
2. Boxes are scored 1 to 5 from the top down
3. Discrepancy scores are calculated for each item (eg 4 − 1 = 3)
4. These 25 discrepancy scores are summed
5. Subtract this total from 100 to give a Compatibility Quotient (CQ) out of 100

Interpretation:

80+ Highly compatible
60–80 Fairly compatible
50–60 Dubious
<50 Incompatible

## PREDICTING LOVER COMPATIBILITY

The less a couple differs on each item the better the long-term compatibility.
For each item please tick the box ☐ that applies to you.

| YOUR HEIGHT | YOUR SEX DRIVE | SEX FIDELITY | PREFERRED RELATIONSHIP |
|---|---|---|---|
| ☐ Tall | ☐ Non-existent | ☐ Essential | ☐ Casual friendship |
| ☐ Above average | ☐ Fairly quiet | ☐ Important | ☐ Lasting friendship |
| ☐ Average | ☐ Average | ☐ Odd lapse OK | ☐ Short-term affair |
| ☐ Below average | ☐ Above average | ☐ Affairs expected | ☐ Intimate long-term |
| ☐ Short | ☐ Insatiable | ☐ Open & swinging | ☐ Marriage |

| YOUR BUILD | FAVOURITE MUSIC | FOREIGN FOOD | IN BED YOU ARE |
|---|---|---|---|
| ☐ Fat | ☐ Rap, reggae | ☐ Can't stand it | ☐ Still a virgin |
| ☐ Ample | ☐ Pop eg top 10 | ☐ Prefer plain food | ☐ Rather inexperienced |

| | | | |
|---|---|---|---|
| ☐ Average | ☐ Easy listening | ☐ OK for a change | ☐ No complaints so far |
| ☐ Slim | ☐ Jazz | ☐ Enjoy most foods | ☐ An experienced lover |
| ☐ Skinny | ☐ Classics, opera | ☐ Prefer foreign | ☐ Really hot stuff |

| **YOUR IQ** | **FAVOURITE TV** | **LIKE PARTIES?** | **YOUR EDUCATION** |
|---|---|---|---|
| ☐ Bright | ☐ Game shows | ☐ Prefer solitude | ☐ Incomplete secondary |
| ☐ Above average | ☐ Soap operas | ☐ Small groups OK | ☐ Completed secondary |
| ☐ Average | ☐ Cops, comedies | ☐ A few parties OK | ☐ Some tertiary |
| ☐ Below average | ☐ Serious dramas | ☐ Fond of parties | ☐ Graduate degree |
| ☐ Dull | ☐ Documentaries | ☐ Love wild parties | ☐ Postgraduate degree |

| **YOUR APPEARANCE** | **CHIVALRY IS** | **SMOKING IS** | **FAVOURITE PHYSICAL ACTIVITY** |
|---|---|---|---|
| ☐ Very attractive | ☐ Outmoded nonsense | ☐ Intolerable | ☐ Relaxed eg in chair |
| ☐ Rather attractive | ☐ Undesirable | ☐ Fairly undesirable | ☐ Mild eg gardening |
| ☐ Average | ☐ OK sometimes | ☐ OK for others | ☐ Moderate eg walking |
| ☐ Rather plain | ☐ Desirable | ☐ You smoke lightly | ☐ Stern eg backpacking |
| ☐ Very plain | ☐ Vital to living | ☐ You smoke heavily | ☐ Strenuous eg football |

| | **DRINKING IS** | **YOUR RELIGION** | **OCCUPATION (planned or actual)** |
|---|---|---|---|
| | ☐ Unacceptable | ☐ Active & committed | ☐ Professional eg doctor |
| | ☐ OK for others | ☐ Some churchgoing | ☐ Business eg manager |
| | ☐ You drink occas | ☐ Private worship | ☐ Clerical eg salesperson |
| | ☐ You drink often | ☐ No worship | ☐ Trades eg mechanic |
| | ☐ You drink to xs | ☐ Anti-religious | ☐ Unskilled eg labourer |

| | **YOUR POLITICS** | **CHILDREN** | **BEST DIVISION OF LABOUR** |
|---|---|---|---|
| | ☐ Far left | ☐ You dislike them | ☐ He works, she stays home |
| | ☐ Left of centre | ☐ Other people's OK | ☐ Her part-time job is OK |
| | ☐ Centre/No interest | ☐ No strong feelings | ☐ Depends on his/her talents |
| | ☐ Right of centre | ☐ May want your own | ☐ She has own job, is indep |
| | ☐ Far right | ☐ Do want your own | ☐ Total equality |

| | **PORNOGRAPHY IS** | **IS MONEY IMPORTANT?** | **IS LIFE UNDER YOUR CONTROL?** |
|---|---|---|---|
| | ☐ Disgusting | ☐ No, can't buy happiness | ☐ Totally yes ) Success mainly |
| | ☐ Prefer to avoid | ☐ Want enough to live | ☐ Mostly yes ) due to effect |
| | ☐ OK sometimes | ☐ Want to be comfy | ☐ In between |
| | ☐ Harmless fun | ☐ Want to be rich | ☐ Mostly no ) Success mainly |
| | ☐ A great turn-on | ☐ Want to be very rich | ☐ Totally no ) due to luck |

# 4

# The chemistry of love

*Love is a hormonal trick.*

Chrissy Iley[1]

When it comes to finding love, says the gambler Sky Masterson in the musical *Guys and Dolls*, he'll be content to leave it to 'chance and chemistry'. By this time, he is in fact already in love with a most unsuitable woman – the naïve Sister Sarah, who devotes her life to saving sinners like him from the evils of drink and gambling. As is the way with musicals, their story looks like having a happy ending ('Marry the man today and change his ways tomorrow'), but is falling in love actually just a matter of chance and chemistry in real life? An ever-growing body of research suggests that, while they may not be the whole answer, such factors certainly play an important part in creating the sensations we recognise as being 'in love', at least in the initial stages of a relationship.

## Hormones and the brain

It is now widely accepted that hormones play a central role in the development of relationships, but which ones are dominant varies during succeeding phases. Initially, it is the sex hormones and pheromones that take centre stage; they are overtaken during the next phase by hormones such as adrenaline and nor-adrenaline, which are experienced as excitement. Then, if the relationship is to be sustained, a third group of hormones starts to predominate. These are bonding chemicals such as oxytocin and vasopressin, and possibly endorphins. The balance of each of these hormones or groups of hormones varies from one individual to another and over time, but their importance is determined by evolution, which, as it must, prioritises procreation and thus gene survival.

The first step in trying to unravel the complex role of hormones is to consider what they are and what they do. Scientists have now identified around 200 different hormones, which are chemicals secreted into the bloodstream by endocrine glands around our bodies and controlled by complex 'feedback' systems involving the brain. These chemicals regulate many vital aspects of our bodily functions, including growth and metabolism, sleep and waking, and many aspects of sex and reproduction. Other chemicals released in the brain, known as neurotransmitters (or chemical messengers), affect perceptions, emotions and the way the brain and nervous system function, while pheromones, sometimes called 'erotic sweat', may be part of the secret of an individual's sexual appeal.

Imbalances in body chemistry can cause not only physical disorders, such as thyroid disease or diabetes, but can also have a profound effect on mood and general wellbeing. Clinical depression, for example, is often related to low levels of the neurotransmitters serotonin and norepinephrine or to disruption in the balance of the various female sex hormones, although experts disagree about the underlying reasons why such disturbances have occurred. The fact that hormones and other chemicals affect us both physically and psychologically largely accounts for the wide and disturbing array of symptoms that we associate with the feeling that we are in love. So just what is going on to create this storm of mixed sensations?

## The first encounter

When you first meet a potential partner, many factors come into play as you sense whether you find them sexually attractive. Some psychologists have proposed that each of us carries in our minds what they call a 'love map' – a term coined by sexologist John Money of Johns Hopkins University.[2] This is a kind of internal template against which we subconsciously measure others to see whether they meet our personal criteria of desirability; it probably developed early in our lives as we built up a picture of our ideal love partner. When we do come into contact with an individual who seems to fit the 'map', our bodies respond by releasing a cascade of chemicals that can leave us spluttering, incoherent and breathless.

Initially, this tumultuous condition is accompanied in the brain by the release of a neurochemical called phenylethylamine (PEA), the effects on mood of which are similar to those caused by amphetamines.[3] In addition, your heart rate increases, your blood pressure rises, you breathe faster, your skin becomes flushed and your palms sweaty, effects that are due to the adrenal glands releasing adrenaline and noradrenaline – stress hormones that are part of the body's 'fight or flight' response to potentially threatening situations. When you are in this heightened state of both physical and emotional arousal, your pupils dilate and your muscle tone increases, you tend to pull your shoulders back and hold your stomach in. All these changes make you seem even more attractive to the other person, even though you are unlikely to notice them on a conscious level. The appeal of dilated pupils is particularly powerful; when people are shown two pictures of the same person, identical except for the fact that one has been doctored to increase pupil size, the altered picture is rated as more attractive.[4]

As this cocktail of chemicals floods your system, the effect is to produce a sensation of euphoria – a kind of natural high – so you feel excited and desperate to see more of the person who creates this stimulating if disturbing array of feelings. As with the drugs that trigger similar responses, the withdrawal effects are unpleasant and often dramatic, leaving you miserable, lethargic and anxious to return to the state of exhilaration that made you feel on top of the world. Many people crave chocolate when they have had a disappointment in their love life, and it may be no coincidence that chocolate contains stimulant chemicals that are similar to PEA. Some researchers are sceptical of the 'chocolate theory of love', since PEA in food is quickly broken down in our bodies and possibly does not reach the brain. Nevertheless, it remains likely that sudden and extreme rises and falls in the levels of these bodily chemicals account for the unmistakable 'emotional roller-coaster' that can turn a normally rational individual into someone they hardly recognise (and don't always like) under the influence of love.[5]

In an attempt to learn more about what goes on in the brains of people in love, researchers at the University of London recruited 17 young men and women who had fallen in love in the previous six to 12 months.[6] Each had their brains scanned to measure changes in blood flow as they looked at a photo of their loved one, then at three friends of the same sex. The scans showed heightened activity in various brain areas when the volunteers looked at their lovers' photos. One was part of an area called the anterior cingulate cortex, which is known to be involved in responding to synthetic drugs that induce feelings of euphoria. Other areas in the basal ganglia region were also particularly active. As well as playing a part in making certain experiences feel rewarding, they are thought to be involved in the process of addiction. Of equal significance, said the researchers, was the fact that certain brain areas were less active when the subjects looked at their lovers' photos: the posterior cingulated gyrus, which is associated with feelings of sadness, and the right pre-frontal cortex, which is often over-active in people suffering from depression.

## Love and obsession

The sense that being in love is a state in which normal brain function is disrupted receives some support from the results of an intriguing study reported in 1999 by Donatella Marazziti and her colleagues at the University of Pisa.[7] The researchers set out to test their hypothesis that there might be similarities in brain chemistry between people who are in love and those suffering from obsessive-compulsive disorder – the irresistible need to continually and unnecessarily repeat actions such as hand-washing or checking things like door and window locks. They tested the blood of 20 students who had recently fallen in love and found that its level of a protein involved in aiding the function of the neurotransmitter serotonin was 40 per cent below normal. This was comparable to the levels found in people with diagnosed obsessive-compulsive disorder. The cells that use this neurotransmitter are located in an area of the brain called the limbic system, which is involved in emotions such as fear, anger, aggression, pain and sexual arousal. Quite what these findings signify is not entirely clear, but they do suggest that at least some of the sensations and behaviour associated with being in love are related to serotonin levels in the brain and, in this respect, are parallel to an obsessional state.

## 'Erotic sweat': the action of pheromones

The role of chemicals called pheromones in sexual attraction has long been a subject for research and discussion among scientists, not to mention companies hoping to market synthetic versions, which would be virtually guaranteed to generate vast profits. Natural pheromones are secreted by the sweat glands in the armpits and groins of both men and women and may be sensed by other people, whether or not they are aware of it. In the absence of deodorants, men and women smell differently, the female smell being described as 'sweet' and the male as relatively musky. But, of course, pheromone effects can also occur without any conscious appreciation of an odour.

People's sensitivity to pheromones varies considerably, as do their reactions to those they can detect. Recent studies of the role of pheromones in human sexual behaviour have been reviewed by David Giles.[8] Among the more interesting studies he described was one by D B Gower of London University, who studied subjects' responses to a group of pheromones called androsterone, which are secreted in underarm sweat. Of those who were able to detect their presence, some people liked the smell, while others were ultra-sensitive to these pheromones and found their odour distinctly unattractive. Other research quoted by Giles was conducted at the University of Northumbria by Andrew Scholey. It looked at the effect of pheromones collected from armpits on the sexual attractiveness ratings of vignettes of individual men and women. The results showed that both men and women rated the sexual attractiveness of a vignette of an opposite sex person more highly in the presence of appropriate pheromones.

Karl Grammer and Astrid Juette at the University of Vienna found similar effects when men were asked to rate photos of women, some of which had been chosen to represent a low level of sexual attractiveness.[9] Higher attractiveness ratings were given in the presence of female pheromones (copulins), the effect being especially pronounced for the photos of women who had originally been rated as relatively unattractive. Thus one of the effects of female pheromones seems to be to make men less discriminating.

These studies were, of course, done in laboratory conditions and it cannot be assumed that the same responses would necessarily occur in real life. Karl Grammer reports that synthetic pheromones did not have the desired effect and indeed were sometimes actually counter-productive, making the wearer feel depressed rather than extra sexy. Other researchers, however, have found synthetic pheromones to be effective. Teams from Brooklyn College, New York and San Francisco State University studied the effects of a synthetic pheromone produced by scientists at the Athena Institute in Pennsylvania, who were also involved in the project. Of 38 young men recruited as subjects, 17 were given an aftershave that, unknown to them, included the chemical. The subjects' sex lives were first assessed for two weeks before the study began. Their sexual activity was then monitored and any differences between those with the 'extra' ingredient in their aftershave and those without assessed. Almost half (41 per cent) of the men in the pheromone group reported a noticeable increase in their sexual activity, compared with only 9.5 per cent in the control group. The 'pheromone' men experienced more kissing and petting as well as an increase in the number of times they had sex.[10]

It seems certain that natural pheromones contribute to sexual attraction in humans as they undoubtedly do in other mammals, although just how and why they do so is not entirely clear. It seems likely that they set off a response in the limbic region of the brain. Women, like other female mammals, are more sensitive to male pheromones at times of peak fertility, which means around the time of ovulation. They also find them more agreeable around this time.[11] Equally, men respond most strongly to pheromones produced by women during the most fertile phases of their menstrual cycle. However, animal studies have shown that the role of pheromones in reproductive behaviour is not simply a matter of stimulus and response and science is still some way from achieving a complete understanding of the part played by these chemicals in human sexual activity.

## The sex hormones

The female sex hormones oestrogen and progesterone and the male sex hormone testosterone are clearly involved in stimulating or depressing the desire for sex. Most women know very well that their levels of desire and receptiveness fluctuate with their menstrual cycle, often peaking around the time of ovulation when oestrogen levels are at their highest and, in some women, increasing just before or after a period. Levels also go up during sex and will generally be higher if a woman is making love on a regular basis. A sex hormone called DHEA (dehydroepiandrosterone), released by the adrenal glands, reaches a level three to five times higher than normal before and during an orgasm and is thought to increase the sex drive. A woman is also likely to be more fertile if she is having regular sex.

Testosterone production surges in boys at puberty and is largely responsible for their tendency to be so preoccupied with sex. Women also produce testosterone in their ovaries and adrenal glands, although in significantly smaller quantities than men, and it is also likely that their sensitivity to it varies. Testosterone is known to be a factor in the strength of the sex drive in women as well as men and, as with oestrogen, production rises to a peak around the time of ovulation. It is interesting to note that testosterone levels drop in men who are involved in a long-term, monogamous relationship – presumably because they no longer have the opportunity to be constantly seeking new sexual partners. It is perhaps a sad reflection on the state of marriage that the same decline in testosterone is observed in long-term prisoners and men who are depressed.

For obvious ethical reasons, much of the research relating to hormones and sexual activity has been conducted in animals rather than human beings. While the results may provide pointers to the likely influence of such hormones on human behaviour, researchers counsel against drawing simplistic conclusions based on assumptions drawn from animal studies. To a greater degree than other animals, humans balance biological impulses driven by their body chemistry with constraints imposed by their intellect and the society they live in. Even if an adult male is biologically programmed to mate with every female within range, his thinking self, not to mention the women concerned or society as a whole, would not generally regard this as acceptable behaviour. Similarly, most women do not confine their sexual activity to times when their hormones decree that they are most likely to conceive and, in any case, hormonal methods of contraception disrupt this natural variation in hormone levels.

## Pleasure and bonding

Oxytocin, a hormone secreted by the pituitary gland at the base of the brain, has long been recognised as one of the factors that triggers the uterus to contract in a pregnant woman and synthetic forms of it are used to induce labour. It is also released during breast-feeding. However, there is evidence that it is released in other circumstances as well and has a significant influence on sexual and emotional responses in both men and women.[12] In addition to its known physical effects – stimulating muscle contraction and increasing nerve sensitivity – oxytocin would seem to have emotional effects, encouraging feelings of closeness and bonding, which is why it has sometimes been called the 'cuddle chemical'.

Its role is not confined to the post-coital phase of love and sex – it is believed to play a part in enhancing the desire for sex in the first place. Levels begin to rise dramatically in both men and women during kissing and, particularly, as they approach orgasm. Ultimately, they may increase to from three to five times the normal as the man ejaculates and possibly even more in a woman if she has an orgasm. It may be that this hormone is responsible, at least in part, for the feeling of euphoria and the sense of real union with your partner after you have had good sex.

This may be connected to the feelings that breast-feeding mothers describe of special closeness to and love for their baby, which may also be related to high levels of oxytocin present during feeding. From an evolutionary point of view, this explanation makes good sense in that oxytocin creates such sensations as a kind of reward for caring for the needy newborn and provides an incentive for the mother to nurture her baby. The same mechanism could be at work between adult sexual partners, encouraging them to stay together so that they may pool resources to look after any offspring that should result from their union.

Helen Fisher suggests that oxytocin is the glue that keeps partners together to care for their offspring once the initial excitement created by sex hormones and neurotransmitters has subsided.[13] It has been observed that women tend to have relatively high levels of this bonding hormone in their blood during their twenties, when their biologically driven impetus to have children is at its peak. Levels decline as child-bearing becomes less of a realistic possibility and the woman's need to retain a provider for her and her offspring becomes correspondingly less intense. Conversely, as men grow older, their sex drive becomes less urgent as testosterone declines and oxytocin may then have a greater influence, steering some, at least, towards a steadier, more committed relationship.

Many of these oxytocin effects are enhanced and prolonged by a chemically related pituitary hormone called vasopressin (sometimes known as adiuretin or ADH, antidiuretic hormone). It also plays a role in regulating metabolism and stimulating lactation. As with oxytocin, levels of vasopressin rise with the approach of orgasm, suppressing other physical sensations such as hunger and concentrating the senses on sexual sensations. From an emotional perspective, vasopressin is thought to enhance feelings of satisfaction and the warmth we feel towards the person we love. Since it is also thought to play a role in generating and preserving memories, it may have something to do with creating those powerful associations, well-known to lovers, between a particular person and a place, a smell or a tune.

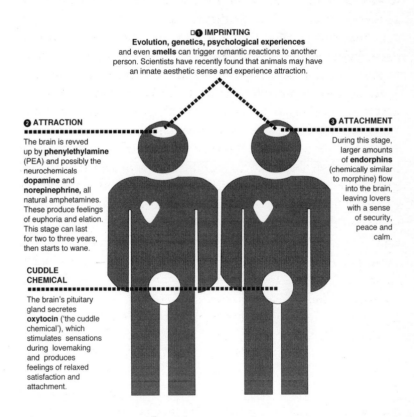

Figure 4.1 Phases of love and the brain chemicals associated with them (from Time magazine, 15 February 1993, based on material from Fisher, 1992)

It is because of the way they affect our feelings towards a lover that oxytocin and vasopressin are seen as being important in sustaining relationships beyond the initial excitement of being in love. The theory is that through the process of evolution humans have developed these and other chemical mechanisms to ensure that we continue to meet the needs of our immature offspring until such time as they can fend for themselves. Nature is effectively 'bribing' us with feelings of love and satisfaction to persuade us not to neglect the necessary task of rearing the next generation and, thus, ensuring the survival of our 'selfish genes'.[14] It has even been suggested that clinical disorders such as autism, which are characterised by an inability to form normal social attachments, may be understood as deficiencies of oxytocin and vasopressin.[15]

Of course, as with other biological explanations for the changing pattern of relationships over time, none of these theories should be taken in isolation. They cannot – and do not – provide a complete explanation of human behaviour. Individuals vary in what they want and how they behave and each of us brings other factors to bear on the way we feel about sex and relationships. We are not slaves to our body chemistry any more than we can deny its influence.

## Kissing

'A kiss is just a kiss… as time goes by' according to pianist and singer Sam in the film *Casablanca* – he of 'Play it again Sam' fame. Wrong, say the scientists. According to Gus McGrouther, who in 1994 conducted a study of the activity in the Department of Plastic Surgery at the Phoenix Research Unit at University College London, an erotic kiss between lovers involves practically every muscle in your body.[16] Using lasers, scanners and electrodes to assess exactly what happens during a kiss, McGrouther and his colleagues found that it is a complex business. Electrical measurements revealed that all 34 facial muscles take part in a kiss, their movements controlled by electrochemical signals from a part of the brain called the facial nerve nucleus. The lips are packed with hypersensitive nerve endings, which send signals back to a relatively large area of the brain's cortex, creating pleasurable sensations and enhancing sexual desire.

As the kiss becomes more exciting, the lips engorge with blood, turning red and becoming swollen like erectile tissue in other parts of the body, like the genitals and nipples. The so-called French kiss, with mouths open and the tongue penetrating the other person's mouth, is more obviously erotic as it parallels the act of sexual intercourse itself. In the process, saliva and sebum are exchanged between the lovers, almost certainly bringing pheromones and bonding chemicals into play, thus enhancing sexual excitement and love.

Since kissing features so largely in our society as a natural, normal and wholly enjoyable aspect of love and sex, and since the lips and facial muscles seem so well equipped for it, it is perhaps surprising that erotic kisses are not universally appreciated. In Polynesian society, for example, lovers opt to touch cheeks or noses – which allows them to breathe in one another's odour. This may be understandable given the chances of passing on disease through mouth-to-mouth kissing, but it is perhaps the need to overcome this basic inhibition that makes kissing such an intimate act.

### Addicted to love?

Recently, there was a flurry of stories in the media about a number of celebrities, including Michael Douglas, reportedly being treated in clinics for 'sex addiction' (although Douglas has since denied this). It was never made entirely clear just what comprised such an addiction or, indeed, whether it was actually curable if it existed, but it is not hard to imagine that it might be real. The sensations, both physical and emotional, associated with being in love – the thrill of the chase and the high of sex itself – are powerful and exciting and are often described in similar terms to the sensations experienced by people who take so-called 'recreational drugs' such as cocaine and amphetamines.

As we have seen, the flood of hormones and neurotransmitters triggered by falling in love and by having sex with a new lover generates a whole range of bodily responses that can leave you feeling like a completely different person. The racing heart, butterflies in the stomach and emotional excitement can make you feel as if you're really alive and on a different plane from that of your ordinary, everyday existence. Chemicals such as adrenaline, noradrenaline and, above all, phenylethylamine, engender a mental 'high', which is comparable to that produced by drugs.[17]

This state does not last for ever and, when the relationship settles on to a more even keel after the first weeks or months, some people miss the euphoria and excitement in the same way as amphetamine or cocaine users miss the 'rush' that these drugs provide. The body adapts to the effects of these natural stimulants and, as with synthetic stimulants, needs ever-increasing amounts to produce and maintain that 'walking on air' feeling. Unfortunately, there are limits to the body's ability to generate substances such as phenylethylamine and a comedown is inevitable eventually. As already noted, phenylethylamine is one of the components of chocolate, but however much of it you gobble up, it doesn't have quite the same effect as the body's own supply.

Regrettably, perhaps, the same kind of decline often sets in with regard to sexual excitement when you have been with the same partner for a while. Few people are able to sustain the intense passion of their first sexual encounters with a lover, although that is not to say that their sex lives will not continue to be satisfying and rewarding for many years to come. Nevertheless, the character of sex is likely to change as the chemistry alters and starts to promote bonding and closeness rather than intoxicating excitement and desire.

According to Michael Liebowitz of the New York State Psychiatric Institute, this settling down is not acceptable to a group of individuals he terms 'attraction junkies'.[18] For them, the rush that comes with falling in love is what matters, and once that initial sense of intoxication begins to fade they tend to abandon the existing relationship and move on to someone new with whom they can rediscover that fizzing feeling. Commitment and closeness hold little appeal for such people because, for them, it is the racing heart, the excitement and euphoria that count, just as it apparently is for those who crave the chemical rush of narcotics. For them, 'love is the drug', as the Bryan Ferry song has it, and they are its addicts.

## A sense of proportion

While there is no denying the physiological effects of what we might call the 'love chemicals', surely there must be more to loving someone than a slavish following of the dictates of body chemistry? For one thing, there are many loving partnerships that grow more slowly and quietly and do not have their origins in the kind of extraordinary sensations we have been considering. Falling in love can just as easily be a matter of gradual exploration and revelation as a sudden explosion and no less genuine as a result. Psychiatrist Mark Goulston of the University of California, Los Angeles, makes an interesting distinction. 'Early love', he says, 'is when you love the way the other person makes you feel. Mature love is when you love the person as he or she is'.[19] It's an important distinction because, when you are buffeted by the emotional highs and lows that are an essential component of being in love, your judgement and perceptions can be radically distorted. You cannot think straight because rationality loses out to excitement and euphoria and you inevitably focus on your own thrilling sensations rather than on the reality of the person who is creating them. Most people know how it feels when the initial obsession fades and stark reality begins to intrude: not every romantic encounter, however initially exciting, culminates in true or lasting love.

So what else matters, besides pure chemistry? There are probably as many answers to that question as there are individual people who love one another and poets, writers and song lyricists have added their contributions through the ages. Whether they are deluded or not, most people believe that they are, in some mysterious fashion, more than just a conglomeration of chemicals and electrical signals. Whatever the scientists may say, they will continue to insist that there is more to human love than chemistry and that it is not merely a 'hormonal trick'.

# 5

# Kinds of loving

*I am attracted to thin, tall, good-looking men who have one common denominator. They must be lurking bastards.*

Edna O'Brien

You only have to read through the pages of personal messages in the papers on Valentine's Day to get an insight into the secret language of lovers. Pet names, mysterious references to in-jokes, song lyrics and poetry are intermingled with passion, sensuality and the despair of those whose love is not requited. Yet if you were to meet the advertisers in person in an everyday situation, you would be unlikely to encounter any clue to the romantic, playful or even passionate impulses that led them to create such messages. Even the most conventional and apparently rational individual may be capable of turning into quite a different person with their partner or lover. This is because romantic love is, in some senses, a throwback to earlier, even childish, modes of behaviour and relating.

## Attachment theory

Proponents of the attachment theory of love believe that there is a direct relationship between the kind of emotional bonds a young child develops with his or her primary care-giver and the love relationships they develop as adults. In his influential books, John Bowlby proposed that babies have an inbuilt need from birth to make emotional attachments because this increases their chances of survival by ensuring that they receive the care they need.[1, 2] The degree to which this need is met influences the way the child develops emotionally through adolescence into adulthood. The more an infant feels able to rely on the primary care-giver (or attachment figure, who is most likely to be the mother) to be there when needed, the more confidence they will have in social situations and relationships with others as adults. Conversely, if the attachment figure cannot be relied on to be responsive to their needs, this will be reflected in the way they approach love relationships as adults. The expectations built up in childhood tend to persist and have a profound effect on an individual's loving relationships throughout their life.

From these ideas other researchers identified three attachment styles, although of course many people will not fit neatly into one or other of them and there is considerable overlap between each.[3] Those with a *secure* attachment style have a generally positive view of themselves and others and are comfortable with emotional closeness and interdependence with a partner. Someone with an *avoidant* attachment style will be reluctant to allow too much intimacy and closeness and find it difficult to trust a partner completely. People whose attachment style is *anxious* want to get as close to their partner as possible and constantly fear losing their love. An individual's basic attachment style is reflected in the way they relate to a love partner in terms of the kind of support they both offer and receive.[4] The person with a secure attachment style is able to seek support from their partner and offer it in return, whereas avoidant types are much less inclined to do this. Unsurprisingly perhaps, it has been shown that securely attached couples tend to be most content with their relationships and have relatively high levels of self-esteem, while those with an anxious style are less well placed in both respects.[5] The avoidant attachment style, and hence difficulties in adult relationships, may sometimes be traced to abusive childhood experiences.[6]

Since the 'template' that shapes adult emotional relationships is built on the basis of childhood experience, it might be inferred that baby talk, pet names, holding hands and other childlike behaviour between lovers are ways of showing and recapturing the loving intimacy they experienced as children.

## Colour combinations

Much research has been dedicated to unravelling the ways in which people behave when they are in love, why they do so and how they differ from one another. While it is clear that there are many different styles of loving, there is no real consensus as to what exactly each consists of nor how they should be defined and distinguished from one another. One of the pioneers in this field was John Lee, whose 1976 book *The Colors of Love* explained to a lay audience his theory that love can be categorised into three fundamental types (analogous to the three primary colours) and three secondary types, which may blend and overlap.[7] According to this analysis, the way you behave towards your lover depends largely on the 'colour' of the love you feel for them. Of course, it is also influenced by the 'colour' of their love for you; if the two conflict, the relationship may be stormy, unhappy or short-lived. In a more recent analysis, Lee outlined eight love styles, drawing up short profiles of the typical attitudes and behaviour attributed to each.

- *Eros*: this type of lover is 'eager to get to know the beloved quickly, intensely – and undressed. They are open-eyed to flaws and potential shortcomings in the beloved, and seek to express their delight in the beloved in verbal and tactile ways'.

- *Ludus*: playful lovers 'feel no special excitement and certainly do not fall in love'. Ludic lovers avoid seeing their partners too often, as a means of keeping things fresh and preventing themselves and their partners from getting 'too involved'. They avoid jealous partners, who spoil the fun of love.
- *Storge*: these lovers 'recoil from an excessive show of emotion in the partner, and prefer to talk about interests they share rather than their feelings for each other... Mutual love is not a goal for life itself, but an aspect of the greater goals of friendship and family'.
- *Mania*: manic lovers 'often appear to have lost their senses, going to absurd extremes to prove their love. Demonstrations of love alternate with times of drawing back to "get control" of themselves, usually without success. Thus manic lovers are led to extreme displays of jealousy, and to demands that their partner show more affection and commitment'.
- *Pragma*: pragmatic lovers 'restrain discussion of commitment and the future until they are more confident they know the partner well. They generally disdain emotional displays and especially jealous scenes, but they appreciate reciprocal signs of thoughtfulness and increasing commitment'.
- *Storgic Eros*: these lovers 'see love as a duty to respond to others. Although pleased by reciprocation, they are not jealous or possessive. Storgic erotic lovers never try to compel their partners to show love or commitment. There is little emphasis on sexual intimacy; gentle, warm feelings are more highly valued'.
- *Ludic Eros*: for this combination style, 'Feelings are expressed in ways that indicate they are not exclusively felt for that particular partner. Jealousy and possessiveness are avoided, and when a relationship ceases to be enjoyable, it is terminated. Love should be a creative experience, and fun for everyone concerned'.

- *Storgic Ludus*: lovers of this type 'feel no special need to be in love with the partner. These lovers feel no jealousy or possessiveness... Feelings are not expressed intensely, nor on a wide range of emotions, and there is never any commitment to a long-range future'.

According to Lee, lovers with the same preferred style get along fine initially, although there is always the danger that the close match will eventually result in boredom. A relationship with a partner whose love style is compatible but not identical may have a better chance of success. Conversely, when there is a major conflict in needs and expectations – as with Ludus and Mania for example – the relationship is likely to be traumatic and difficult, which is not to say that such combinations are at all rare!

You can have fun – and perhaps gain some insight into yourself – by speculating as to how and where you, as well as any past or present partners, fit into this classification system. In fact, most people will probably discover that, if they have had more than one love relationship in their lives, they will have experienced love of more than one 'colour'. Intuitively, it seems likely that we will experience more ludic, erotic and manic loves when young and more storgic and pragmatic relationships when older.

## Friends, then lovers?

While it is common for passionate love to cool into friendship, to what extent is it possible for friends to become successful lovers? In Chapter 1, we noted that Zick Rubin devised a questionnaire to distinguish between liking and loving, which subjects answered with respect to a partner and to a friend of the same sex.[8] This showed that while people used terms such as admirable, worthy of respect and similarity to themselves when assessing friends, when it came to lovers they placed the emphasis on needing to be with that person, wanting to help them – even at their own expense – and being absorbed in and caring intimately for them. Interestingly, women tended to like the men they loved rather more than the men liked them.

Studies of cross-gender friendships have found many of these attitudes prevailing towards friends of the opposite sex. However, while both men and women say they gain a lot from such friendships, including intimacy and affection, they frequently choose to keep them separate from their romantic relationships.[9] One study actually found that romance and sex were often destructive of such friendships.[10] Almost half of the people in this survey said their friendships had ended because they turned into romantic relationships that didn't work out, because one or both began a romance with someone else or because one of the pair wanted a romantic relationship while the other did not. Some of these problems were explored in the film *When Harry Met Sally*, in which a long, close and intimate friendship is dramatically unbalanced when the couple have sex. The experience destroys their former ability to be easy and comfortable with one another until, as is the way with romantic comedies, they finally get it together as loving partners as well as friends.

## Personality and love style

Love styles have been linked to personality types. For example, Martin Davies asked 127 college students to take the Eysenck Personality Questionnaire to measure their levels of extraversion, neuroticism and psychoticism. They also completed the Love Attitudes Scale, which sorted them into one of Lee's primary and secondary love colours.[11] Davies found relationships between extraversion, Ludus and Eros and between neuroticism and Mania, and a negative relationship between neuroticism and Pragma. He also reported negative associations between psychoticism, Agape and Storge but a positive relation with Ludus. These findings suggest that certain factors in your personality influence the love style that you prefer. They further suggest that more balanced personalities favour the cooler colours of love, such as Pragma, Agape and Storge.

The idea that the hotter love colours are indicative of emotional maladjustment is supported by a recent study by John Worobey.[12] He measured various temperamental traits such as anger, distress, sociability and level of activity in his subjects, who were 81 men and 163 women, all around the age of 20 and students at a university in the north-eastern United States. They were asked to complete questionnaires designed to assess their preferred love style, using Lee's six original colours. On the temperament scales, men tended to score higher than women on anger, while women were more prone to distress. Interestingly, Ludus was the least popular love style, although men favoured it slightly more than women, who scored more highly on Storge and Pragma. Women typically believed themselves to be more emotional than men, and more interested in friendship rather than game playing as a basis for romantic relationships. However, the study found that high levels of emotionality (shown by high scores of distress and fearfulness) were the best predictors of preferred love styles. Among the women, the higher scorers tended towards Mania and Agape (fraternal love), while the men were more likely to favour Eros, Mania and Agape. Worobey concluded that temperament is important in predicting which type of love an individual prefers.

Worobey has also related temperament and love style to eating disorders in college women.[13] Obsessive and game-playing love styles were related to dieting and bulimia, while fear and anger were related to bulimia and oral control. Hence, temperament, love relationships and eating problems are interdependent in complex ways. (In this context, dieting referred to pathological food avoidance and preoccupation with shape; bulimia included food preoccupation and body disturbances and oral control referred to self-control with respect to food and acknowledgement of social pressure to gain weight.)

Nancy Grote and Eileen Frieze looked at love styles in relation to the length of time partnerships had lasted.[14] They asked a group of 581 people, aged between 45 and 47, who had been married for an average of 18 years, about their perceptions of how they had felt at the beginning of the relationship with their partner, as well as their current feelings. Overall, responses showed that both men and women rated erotic and ludic love as having been stronger at the beginning of the marriage. Men whose love was agapic said that their feelings had grown in strength over time. Friendship-based love (Storge) was perceived as having remained at the same level over the duration of the marriage. There was more disagreement about the ways in which women and men viewed their experience of love at the beginning of their relationships than in the ways they viewed them currently. The degree to which the perceptions of both sexes had shifted over time with regard to all four types of love was reflected in the level of satisfaction with the current state of the relationship. Some couples had grown towards mutual friendship while others had diverged and hence spent more time apart and engaged in extra-marital relations.

Common sense would suggest that an individual's earliest experience of an adult couple's relationship – usually that of their parents – would have an influence on their own attitudes and expectations when it comes to forming love relationships of their own. There is evidence for this from a study by Susan Sprecher and colleagues, which compared the love styles of two groups of students, one whose parents were divorced and the other whose parents had remained together.[15] Among the women, those with divorced parents were more likely to have an avoidant attachment style and less likely to have a secure one. They were also less likely to have a preferred love style that was pragmatic, agapic or manic, and generally had a less idealistic view of romantic love. However, when the researchers took account of the difference between those whose parents' marriages were happy and those whose marriages, though intact, were unhappy, most of the differences between the two groups of women studied were found to be actually differences between those with happily married and those with divorced parents. In other words, divorce was not the critical factor, but rather happiness in the parental marriage. Men whose parents were divorced were more likely to have Eros as their preferred love style, but this was even more the case with men whose parents had not divorced but were unhappy together. Such research could be taken as support for the argument that it is better for unhappy couples to separate than to stay together for the sake of the children.

## Triangular love theory

Robert Sternberg has proposed a three-way classification of love in which love can be represented by a triangle, with the three points consisting of passion, intimacy and decision/commitment.[16] By combining each of these components with one another in every way, you arrive at eight possible variations of love.

The three main components of the triangle are categorised by Sternberg as follows:

- *Passion*: comprising sexual desire and consummation as well as romantic feelings; a sense of enhanced self-esteem and sometimes feelings of dominance or submission in relation to the partner.

- *Intimacy*: feelings of closeness, mutual understanding and communication, of being bonded emotionally to a partner. It also implies giving and receiving emotional support and putting a high value on the loved one and wanting to promote their wellbeing.
- *Decision/commitment*: in the short term, this means deciding that you love someone and, in the long term, that you are committing yourself to that love. The two may well go together but need not necessarily do so. You may feel committed to your partner even though you do not actually have feelings of love towards them and vice versa.

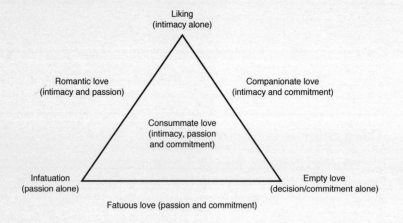

Figure 5.1 Sternberg's triangular view of love (from Sternberg and Barnes, 1988)

This three-dimensional view of the structure of love has received support from studies using a statistical classification technique called factor analysis.[17]

Combinations of Sternberg's primary elements may range from *consummate* love (intimacy, passion and commitment) at one extreme, to *empty* love (decision/commitment only) or *infatuation* (passion only) at the other. Sternberg has identified eight possible ways in which the three elements might be combined in specific relationships and suggested that analysing them in this way may help to predict the future course of a relationship. For example, a partnership based on a single element has a less healthy prognosis. Intimacy alone tends to result in close friendship without passion or a sense of commitment to one's partner. Passion may be the driving force in many instances of 'love at first sight' and might be more realistically categorised as infatuation rather than love. As there is usually no intimacy based on close knowledge of the other person, this kind of 'love' often fades before commitment is possible, although there are exceptions. Decision/commitment, according to Sternberg, may be all that survives of some long relationships that originally incorporated other elements – as with a couple who end up staying together for practical reasons, such as shared property or fear of loneliness, although they no longer feel very much at all for one another. He does point out, however, that where commitment is the basis on which a relationship is founded – such as a traditional arranged marriage – love may grow as the couple become closer and want to make it work.[18]

Romantic love, according to the triangular theory, is based on passion and intimacy but without there necessarily being any idea of a long-term commitment. This is often the case in younger people who fall in love without any immediate plans to settle down, or in an affair between two people who cannot commit themselves to each other because they have ties elsewhere. Companionate love, a combination of intimacy and commitment, may often be long lasting, even though passion may be lacking or only a relatively minor element. Many long marriages take this form when early passion has diminished or disappeared. What the couple still share is enough to make them remain together happily. Love without genuine intimacy is likely to have a much less happy outcome in the longer term – passion and commitment may feature in whirlwind romances but as the couple get to know one another and the element of passion fades, they may come to realise that they have made a mistake. By this time, splitting up is usually a painful process.

Sternberg takes the analogy of the love triangle further to shed light on the way in which each partner views the relationship, how reality compares with their ideal and the extent to which the two people's perceptions coincide. For this purpose he uses the size and shape of each person's triangle – size representing the intensity of love and shape the balance of the three elements. Both partners will have triangles representing their view of the relationship, plus a real and an ideal triangle representing the behaviour of their partner. When these triangles are not 'congruent', that is to say they diverge widely from one another, one or other partner (or both) is likely to become dissatisfied. It is also important for each individual to act in a way that conforms with the size and shape of the triangles. The most crucial aspect here is that each person must act in such a way as to reflect their real feelings of intimacy, passion and commitment and keep those feelings alive. This obviously implies that people – and relationships – change over time and that their actions have an important influence on the course of such changes. In other words, regardless of whatever elements were combined when the relationship began, the balance is likely to shift over time. Developing an awareness of the interplay of the various elements and their relative importance may help couples to make adjustments that will strengthen and preserve their relationship.

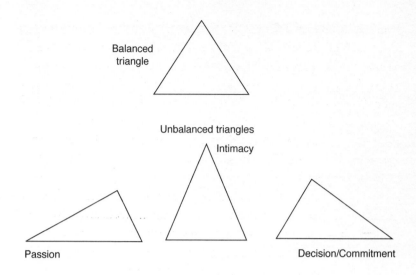

Balanced triangle

Unbalanced triangles

Intimacy

Passion

Decision/Commitment

Figure 5.2 An example of Sternberg's incongruent couples (from Sternberg and Barnes, 1988)

Sternberg's triangular model of love has inspired many research studies and gained much empirical support. For example, one recent study looked at the way intimacy, passion and commitment were perceived within their relationships by 79 couples who were questioned about their subjective experience and communication of these elements. The results showed that these couples experienced intimacy in a range of different ways: openness, affection, supportiveness, togetherness and quiet company. Passion was expressed as sex and romance; commitment as supportiveness, expressions of love, fidelity, constancy and consideration and devotion. The researchers, Peter Marston and colleagues, concluded that Sternberg's three elements formed overlapping clusters in the subjective experience of lovers.[19] Although Lee's colours of love are broadly descriptive and appealing to lay readers, Sternberg's three-way classification probably carries much the same information in a simpler form.

## Personality plus...

If, as this and other research implies, intimacy is one of the more important factors in determining the way a relationship develops and whether it will last, are some people more capable of achieving it than others? Karen and Kenneth Dion have argued that certain personality traits make individuals more or less prone to develop the kind of intimacy that they see as integral to romantic love.[20] Allied to this is the attitude that a person takes towards feeling dependent on a lover. The Dions have conducted studies that related the level of defensiveness and self-esteem of their subjects, as measured by their replies to a range of questionnaires, to the subjects' experiences of romantic love. Among those classified as having high self-esteem and self-acceptance, romantic encounters appeared to happen more often, whereas highly defensive individuals reported fewer such experiences. Yet those whose self-esteem was found to be relatively low seemed to have more intense relationships, which they described as irrational and uncontrollable. The highly defensive people were generally more guarded and less open and, in general, held a more cynical view of love.

In another study, the Dions assessed subjects' self-actualisation – their level of positive mental health, sense of achievement and of having fulfilled their potential – as well as their degree of overall satisfaction with their love lives.[21] Those with high self-actualisation scores were inclined to be more satisfied with either a current or past relationship and to be more intensely involved and open than those with lower scores. However, self-actualised people were more realistic in their expectations and seemed to show lower levels of need and caring for their lovers.

Summarising all their studies, the Dions suggest that people who place a high value on control and show high levels of defensiveness may feel ambivalent about the prospect of increasing intimacy and dependence as a love affair develops. They may avoid full involvement for fear of losing control. Those who are most able to accept themselves as they are, while they may find love a fulfilling experience, may depend less on their partner emotionally than those with less confidence in themselves.

## A Western ideal?

Another aspect of romantic relationships investigated by the Dions is the possible role played by culture in creating our expectations of love.[22] In particular, they reviewed various studies that looked at the values and beliefs on the subject of love and long-term partnerships held by Chinese people and compared the findings with those relating to Americans. They cite the work of Francis Hsu, in which American culture is defined as 'individual-centered', with great emphasis placed on the emotional content of a relationship, whereas Chinese culture is 'situation-centered', whereby emotions are less intense and regarded as having less importance.[23] Hsu summarises this distinction in terms of questions a person of each nationality might ask themselves about a potential or actual love affair: 'An American asks, "How does my heart feel?" A Chinese person asks, "What will other people say?"' Hsu ascribes these differences to the fact that intimate family relationships continue to play a much larger role in the lives of adults in China than in the USA; Americans (and by implication, people in other Westernised societies) must look outside the family to form close and intimate bonds with their peers. Although this work was originally reported in the early 1980s, the attitudes it discusses developed from deep-rooted cultural ideas, and recent changes in parts of Chinese society seem unlikely to have closed the gap.

A study at the University of Miami by Clyde and Susan Hendrick found that students from an Oriental background seemed to favour love styles based on Lee's concepts of pragmatic or storgic love rather than erotic love when compared to students from a white, non-Hispanic background.[24] This is consistent with the idea of Chinese attitudes being relatively selfless compared to those of Anglo-American society.

Early investigations into the importance ascribed to romantic love and marriage in non-industrialised societies such as India (as it then was) and Burma suggested that love was not considered particularly important. In fact, the Indian male students surveyed by G A Theodorson back in 1965 seemed relatively unromantic as well as uninterested in marriage, living as they did in a society where arranged marriage was the norm and the level of economic development relatively low.[25] Presumably, the Indian students did not waste time agonising over whom they were going to marry because they had little or no choice in the matter. In China, people are more likely to aspire to marriage with partners who can offer practical advantages, such as a good income, rather than with someone for whom they feel romantic love. For many Chinese, the Western idea of love appears socially threatening or even illicit, rather than being regarded as a sound basis for marriage.[26]

To most people in Westernised societies, the idea that a happy marriage might be based on anything other than the mutual love of the couple concerned would appear incredible, if not actually repellent. This reluctance to consider an arranged marriage is shared by the majority of young men and women of Asian backgrounds who have been brought up in the West – occasionally resulting in the kind of inter-generational conflict played out in the film *East is East*. Yet in other parts of the world, especially the Indian subcontinent, arranged marriages have been the norm for many generations and, in terms of the longevity of the partnerships at least, would be regarded by many of the couples concerned as a success.

But what of the marital satisfaction of such couples – is it greater or less than that expressed by couples whose marriages were based on love? Paul Yelsma and Kuriakose Athappilly surveyed 53 Indian and 31 American couples in arranged and love marriages to assess their degree of satisfaction and the level of communication between the partners.[27] As far as marital satisfaction was concerned, they found that the Indian couples who had had arranged marriages rated it more highly than did either the Indian or the American couples in love marriages. The latter considered that all types of communication – including sexual – greatly influenced how satisfied they were with their relationships; this factor was deemed less important by those in Indian arranged marriages. The authors suggest that submissiveness, together with careful selection of marital partners and the amount of external support available to the wife are significant factors in determining the amount of marital satisfaction felt by couples in arranged marriages.

Arranged marriages are uncommon in Western countries, but one exception is the mass marriages of members of the Unification Church to partners chosen by its leader, the Reverend Sung Myung Moon. One such event, which took place in 1982, was the subject of a three-year follow-up study by Marc Galanter.[28] Using information from 209 people from the 2,057 married in the ceremony, Galanter found that 95 per cent were still active members of the church and 81 per cent remained married to the partner chosen for them by their leader a year before the ceremony. However, the results of psychological tests showed that the individuals concerned had lower scores for wellbeing than members of the general population, and any who did not conform to the church's expectations seemed particularly distressed. Those who remained closely affiliated with the sect seemed to cope better with psychological problems arising from their unconventional marriages and were thus more likely to conform to the behavioural norms expected of them.

# 6

# Gender wars

*Love is our ancestors whispering in our ears.*

Michael Mills[1]

Most men and women are looking for love. But are they looking for the same thing? It was Jane Austen's Emma who observed of the difference between the sexes, 'One half of the world cannot understand the pleasures of the other'. So just how far do the cluster of attitudes, behavioural and personality traits that make us recognisably male or female – our gender roles as psychologists call them – influence what we are looking for and how we behave in our relationships? And can men and women ever understand each other or, as Austen suggested, are they forever doomed to pursue their separate paths to pleasure?

## Different shopping lists

Whether or not we ever put it into words, most of us have a mental checklist of the attributes we desire in a mate. Few people ever go so far as to write their list down, still less make it public, but whenever we meet a potential partner we are mentally marking off the points with a series of mental ticks and crosses to see how they measure up.

Evidence from dozens of studies conducted at different times and in different countries and cultures confirms that, although men and women may agree on desirable personal qualities such as kindness, understanding, intelligence, health and a pleasing personality, they differ on what they rate as the most important criterion. Men value physical attractiveness more highly than women, while earning power is more important to women.[2]

Back in 1939 US psychologists asked men and women to rate 18 characteristics from irrelevant to indispensable.[3] While women did not view earning power as indispensable they did rate it as important. Men by contrast rated it as desirable but not very important. Follow-up studies mirrored the finding in the next two decades.[4,5] We might expect that economic and social changes that have increased the potential earning power of many women might make the earning power of a prospective partner less important to them. In fact, the opposite appears to be the case. When very high-earning American women were asked how much they would want their ideal partner to earn, they placed much more emphasis on a good income than women who earned a modest living.[6] In addition, the well-off women wanted their men to be well educated and professionally qualified, to have high social status, to be tall, independent and self-confident. By contrast, wealthy men placed little emphasis on the wealth and social power of their female partners. Similar conclusions regarding income were reached by another study of female students who would expect to earn well once qualified. They placed more emphasis on the ability of potential partners to be financially successful than did those women with lower earning expectations.[7] Thus the relative earning power of women does not account for the importance they put on wealth in their prospective partners.

In his cross-cultural study cited above, David Buss found that the men in all 37 societies examined preferred their wives to be younger than themselves, although the preferred age gap differed from one or two years in Scandinavia to six or seven in Nigeria and Zambia. Women, on average, preferred to marry men around three and a half years older than themselves. Data on actual marriages collected for this study confirmed that these preferences were generally put into practice, with the majority of husbands being older than their wives. This suggests that the highly publicised celebrity partnerships between older, successful men and younger, beautiful women are only reflecting in an extreme form the choices made by Mr and Ms Average.

Given the correlation between age and income this finding adds further fuel to the argument that, despite all the changes of the past 30 or so years, women still assess future marital partners on the basis of their ability to bring home the bacon. Young women are, of course, at a premium as far as men are concerned because women are most fertile when young and so evolution has determined that youth and beauty are more closely tied in women than in men. However, Buss found that both men and women in all the cultures he studied still valued personal qualities over looks or earning power, so there is hope for those who are not young, rich or beautiful.

Buss asked his male and female subjects to choose from a list of 32 desirable personality traits in a partner. The top seven, averaged across cultures, were:

1.  Kind and understanding
2.  Intelligent
3.  Exciting personality
4.  Healthy
5.  Emotionally stable and mature
6.  Dependable character
7.  Pleasing disposition.

Sure enough, males all over the world ranked good looks (eighth in the overall world list) higher than females and females ranked good financial prospects (ninth in the overall world list) higher than males. In non-Western countries like China, India, Taiwan and Iran virginity or chastity also scored highly, but was rated as less important in the Netherlands, Sweden and Norway, well known for their permissive attitudes towards sex. In those cultures where virginity or chastity was valued it was rated as more important by men than women.

## Single, white, female WLTM

One of the most interesting manifestations of a perfect partner schema is the lonely hearts column, where men and women list the attributes they are seeking in a partner. Take this selection from British newspaper *The Guardian*'s 'Soulmates' column[8]:

Women seeking men
Tall F 32. I am ready for a loving, committed r/ship with a gentle strong man. Fun-loving and outgoing

Happy, indpt profess F 40, 5' 7", into travel, walking, books, cinema & R4 WLTM M, sim ints

Pretty, dynamic, self-aware F 36 seeks energetic M 30–45, with intelligence and sensitivity, for hill-walking adventures and deep discussions

Eternal optimist 36. Fit, attract, individual, indpt, into self-aware people, white wine, swimming, cycling, art, film, commitment... & maybe you

Men seeking women
Intellig, kind, confident, medium-built attract M 35, 6' 0" seeks slim, attract, intellig, warm brunette F 18–34 for f/ship

Uncompromising lecturer, young 50, 5' 10", honest, awaits slim, pretty, nurturant woman

The lonely hearts columns are interesting because they highlight the expectations of men and women looking for a mate. This is reflected both in the qualities that men and women advertisers choose to hook a mate – that is, the qualities they claim for themselves – as well as in those attributes they say they are looking for in a partner. Perhaps because *Guardian* readers like to think of themselves as progressive – and tend to be slightly older than average – there are fewer ads from men blatantly spelling out desired vital statistics such as age, figure type and hair colour and fewer from women seeking well-heeled males, but the subtext is there, nevertheless.

Just as the US presidency usually falls to the taller candidate, many studies show that women prefer tall to short men as potential partners. In one study short men were deemed undesirable for either short- or long-term partnerships.[9] Studies of the personal ads appear to back this up. A study carried out by US psychologists in 1978 among women who listed height as one of the attributes they were seeking found that 8 out of 10 wanted a man who was at least 6 feet tall.[10] This illustrates the 'cardinal rule' of dating – that the male partner be taller than the female. It is no doubt connected with the fact that taller men are more successful economically and perceived as dominant.[11]

Much of the research into the qualities people seek in a partner has concentrated on long-term relationships, but there is some evidence that different criteria may apply when it comes to picking a short-term partner, particularly as far as men are concerned. In the Buss and Schmitt study, men rated sexual promiscuity and experience as desirable in a short-term mate, although not in a prospective long-term partner; women did not consider these desirable qualities in either situation. Physical attractiveness was more important for both men and women in a short-term as compared with a long-term partner, although men felt more strongly about this than did women.

Men were more reluctant than women to consider a short-term relationship with someone who appeared to be looking for commitment, while women were more wary than men of even a short-term relationship with someone who already had a partner.

An earlier study found that men and women asked to list the qualities they wanted in a long-term and a casual sexual partner largely agreed on the criteria for a long-term mate.[12] In fact the women made few distinctions between the qualities they were seeking in either situation, whereas the men placed much greater emphasis on physical characteristics when listing their criteria for a short-term sexual partner. Other researchers have confirmed this finding with regard to selectivity: men, it seems, are less fussy about the qualities they seek in a short-term sexual relationship than are women, who tend to be more discriminating in their choice of partner, whether they expect the relationship to last or not. Instinctively, perhaps, they seem to be aware that even a brief encounter could have long-term consequences by resulting in pregnancy.

## Playful men, serious women

When men and women have found the object of their affection, do they love in the same way? Despite the success of Mills & Boon romances and historical novels in which the heroine is swept off her feet by a dashing stranger, it seems that the conventional wisdom that women are the more romantic sex is misguided. Survey after survey suggests that women are much more caring and practical in their approach, opting for storgic and pragmatic love styles as defined by John Lee, while men are more drawn towards passionate (erotic) or game-playing (ludic) love styles. US sociologists Terry Hatkoff and Thomas Lasswell suggest this is because women have traditionally been able to control the choice of partner, 'being able to string suitors along while deciding whether to accept or decline their advances or their marriage proposals', and thus have more need to be rational in love.[13] It could be that as women have less financial need for a partner they will become more playful in their approach, but it remains true to some extent that love is a game for men but more of a career for women.

Research also shows that below the age of 20 women fall in love earlier and more often than men. However, once past this age men fall in love more easily and women fall out of love sooner. Studies show that, contrary to received wisdom, women are the stronger sex when it comes to ending a relationship and are much more likely to take the initiative in calling it a day. They are also less likely to report nostalgia, depression or loneliness following the end of a love affair or relationship.[14]

Connected with the male preference for playful love styles mentioned above is another striking difference between men and women. This is the tendency for men to seek novelty in their partners, while women (relatively speaking) are in search of consistency. This has been documented in many different ways, one of which is to look at the differing sexual fantasies of men and women.[15] The diagram below shows the proportion of sexual fantasies devoted to each of four popular themes: sex with a stranger, sex with a famous (identified) person, group sex and homosexuality. While men and women do not differ appreciably in the proportion of fantasy devoted to sex with strangers and homosexual experiences, men are significantly more attracted to group sex, whereas women are more drawn towards sex with a famous man.

This is exactly what evolutionary theory would predict. Men seek multiple partners so as to distribute their genes more widely, while women are concerned with the quality of the man who sires their offspring and his capacity to help provide for them. This difference is so fundamental that it will be addressed more fully in Chapter 8.

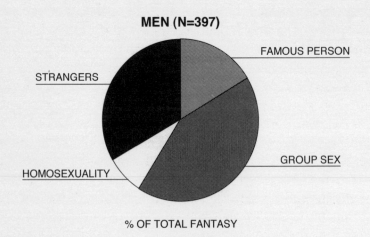

% OF TOTAL FANTASY

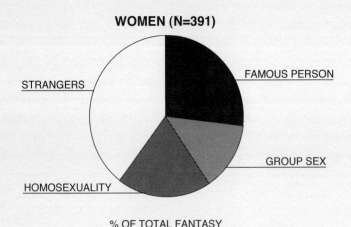

% OF TOTAL FANTASY

Figure 6.1 The differences between male and female sexual fantasies (from Wilson, 1997)

## Nature or nurture?

What accounts for these differences in men and women's templates of an ideal partner and the ways in which they seek to attract him or her? In the 1988 film *Who Framed Roger*

*Rabbit?* the voluptuous Jessica Rabbit drawls, 'I'm not bad really. I'm just drawn that way'. Evolutionary psychologists attribute the differences in what men and women want to the way they are drawn – in other words, to innate differences in the genes and biology of the two sexes. Over millions of years the survival of a female's genes depended on her being attracted to males who could successfully fend off enemies, look after her and provide for their offspring, while survival of the male's genes depended on seducing multiple, young, healthy females who would be able to reproduce. Even though sociologically, medically and in virtually every other way the world has changed beyond all recognition in the past 100 years or so our basic biology hasn't yet caught up, so that men still look for a young, fecund mate while women seek good providers. A few decades are a mere pittance within the evolutionary time scale.

Sociologists counter the evolutionary view by attributing differences in the sexes' mate choices not to biology but to culture and the constraints imposed by the way a particular society is organised. This might imply that, as social organisation changes, women will begin to seek different qualities in their partners. In the past, say the sociologists, because of their primary role as childrearers and the lack of access to resources of their own women were satisfied if a man supported her financially and treated her with kindness. It was taken for granted – as it still is in some upper-class circles – that men would have affairs and, provided they were discreet, nothing was said. However, it might be expected that today's high-powered, high-earning women would be less willing to settle for such an imperfect deal now they have a choice. The example of certain high-profile women suggests that this may be so: for example, Madonna, who chose her personal trainer, Carlos Leon, to father her first child. It could be said that she was exercising her freedom to pick a handsome young man whom some would consider an unsuitable choice by conventional standards. (However, it is worth noting that Madonna's subsequent choice of father for her second child was the film director Guy Ritchie – who is financially more successful and of higher status than her first choice.) Such women might also be expected to be less willing than their mothers and grandmothers to turn a blind eye to a partner's sexual indiscretions.

It was the poet Lord Byron who famously remarked, 'Love of man's life is a thing apart, 'tis woman's whole existence'. Even in today's two-income, two-career families, surveys continue to show that women still take most of the responsibility for the traditionally female emotional work of looking after a relationship. The difference is neatly pointed up in best-selling books such as Helen Fielding's *Bridget Jones's Diary*, with its obsessive recording of weight loss, calories and men. As marriage guidance counsellor Jill Burrett has noted:

> You only have to listen to young adults chatting socially (say on a bus or train) to notice how groups of girls tend to be talking about their boyfriends, whereas boys are talking about study or sporting interests. Women seem to talk to other women as if their relationships are their priority, as if they define themselves in terms of their partners. Men often seem to be talking to other men about women in the language of successful conquests. Girls, it seems, are still practising their relationship sensitivity, boys mastery of their world outside relationships![16]

## The influence of feminism

Sigmund Freud, the father of psychoanalysis, famously asked, 'What do women want?', and since then dozens of researchers have attempted to answer his question. Feminist writers of the 1960s, 70s and 80s weighed in with the view that if there were more equality between the sexes, if men became more open emotionally, getting in touch with their feelings and played a more equal role in housework and childcare, many of the disparities that dog relations between the sexes would disappear. Unfortunately it seems they were wrong. In fact, there is evidence that women who adopt feminist attitudes towards relationships experience more rather than less dissatisfaction. A study of the relationships between sex role attitudes and marital dissatisfaction received replies from 809 women to a questionnaire published in a popular women's magazine.[17] The survey used several ways of assessing respondents' sex role attitudes, including gender-biased cartoons and the Kipnis Marital Power Questionnaire, which assesses techniques of exercising power within a relationship. The women were also asked to rate their degree of happiness with their partner and to give details of how frequently they made love.

The measurement of feminist attitudes was based on an 18-point list with a choice of five responses ranging from 'strongly agree' to 'strongly disagree':

1. Men have held power for too long.
2. Beauty contests are degrading to women.
3. Children of working mothers are bound to suffer.
4. Wives who don't work should do all the housekeeping.
5. Women should be given equality of pay.
6. Women should be given preference in hiring and promotion until past injustices are corrected.
7. Most men are chauvinists.
8. Women are naturally better suited to the job of childrearing.
9. Women should make an effort to be attractive to men.
10. Husbands should always do an equal share of household chores.

11. Women's Lib will change the world for the better.
12. Employers should be free to prefer a man if they think the job calls for a man.
13. Only through following her own career can a woman find fulfilment.
14. Women's Libbers are usually just man-haters.
15. Equal pay for women is at present an unrealistic aim.
16. Men should spend an equal amount of time in childcare duties.
17. Chivalry and romance are threatened by Women's Lib.
18. In many respects women have it easier than men already.

(Note that half the statements represent feminist views and half express a traditional viewpoint – in which case scoring was reversed.)

The results showed that those women whose responses to the list revealed that they held strong feminist views were less likely to be satisfied with their relationships, both in general and with respect to their sex lives. They tended to have sex less frequently than more traditional women and were more likely to use confrontation than accommodation when there was conflict with a partner. Interestingly, however, the most highly traditional, 'domestic' women, who used emotional manipulation to get their way in conflict situations, were also more likely to say they were unhappy in their marriage. It seems that, as in most things, there is a balance to be struck which constitutes the happy medium.

### The men's movement

While individual men have responded in a variety of ways to the challenges posed by feminism – some by ignoring or criticising the movement, others by trying to adapt themselves to become New Men or turning into 'lads' – there has also been an emergence of campaigns and philosophies targeted specifically at men. Prominent among the leaders of such new approaches is the American poet Robert Bly, author of *Iron John*[18] and founder of the seminars and programmes associated with it. He has proposed that many men alive today (primarily in the industrialised Western countries, and particularly the USA) have been adversely emotionally affected by the absence of fathers as role models who can initiate them into the adult world. He suggests that, whereas in the past, fathers were often away from the family for what he calls 'noble' reasons such as fighting a war, they are now more likely to be absent because they have abandoned the family, often for a new partner. Thus instead of idealising the absent father as they once did those who had gone off to serve a cause, young men today justifiably feel abandoned and embittered by the desertion of their male parent. The result of this, claims Bly, is a generation of men who have been unable to grieve for their loss or to express (or even feel) their true emotions and who are therefore unable to make stable, loving relationships themselves. One of his solutions to this problem has been to organise 'gatherings' of men, run by 'mentors', in order to give the emotionally deprived men opportunities to experience physical challenges, bond with other men both of their own age and older, learn to share and express their emotions and to benefit from the help and support of mentors who function as 'substitute dads'.

While sceptics have mocked such events as being little more than tree-hugging, drum-beating displays of childish machismo and pastiches of an illusory 'noble savagery', Bly has claimed that his approach is effective – and his books certainly found an enthusiastic audience. Another attempt to help alienated men to rediscover the joys and responsibilities of family life was the 'Promises' movement in the USA, in which thousands of men joined marches whose leaders aimed to regenerate participants' confidence in themselves as partners and fathers. Such movements have not taken off in the same way elsewhere, but many men have expressed their feelings of loss and injustice at what they see as enforced separation from their children following divorce. Many members or organisations like Families Need Fathers feel the legal system is biased against them and work towards reclaiming their right to be involved with their children. Changes in social and family structures have certainly created a large army of emotionally wounded individuals who no longer have a clear idea of their role within society.

## From different planets?

New Man, the media label for a male who tries to be more caring and sharing, has become a joke. In fact, in recent years we've seen a resurgence of male values in the cult of the 'lad' and his female counterpart 'the ladette', embodied by TV personalities such as Zoë Ball and Denise van Outen. So is there any hope for a better understanding or are men and women doomed to continue to misunderstand one another?

There is evidence that, despite – or even perhaps because of – increases in equality over the past 30 years, male/female relationships continue to be dogged by differences in the way the sexes communicate and express themselves. The runaway success of books such as John Gray's *Men are from Mars, Women are from Venus*[19] would seem to reinforce the perception that men and women still find it difficult to communicate effectively with each other, to the point where readers accept Gray's idea that they may as well come from different planets. The fact that this book and others by the author on the same theme sell so well is surely testament to people's desire to seek solutions, although it would be revealing to know how many of the millions who have bought the book since it was first published in 1993 were women and how many were men – since books of this kind are usually bought mainly by women.

Gray's premise, which essentially popularises research done by evolutionary psychologists and those studying communication styles, is that men's and women's fundamentally different values underpin the way they communicate and are responsible for many of the misunderstandings that arise between them. Women (Venusians), asserts Gray, 'value love, communication, beauty and relationships. They spend a lot of time supporting, helping, and nurturing one another. Their sense of self is defined through their feelings and the quality of their relationships. They experience fulfilment through sharing and relating'. Men (Martians), on the other hand, 'value power, competency, efficiency, and achievement. They are always doing things to prove themselves and develop their power and skills. Their sense of self is defined through their ability to achieve results. They experience fulfilment primarily through success and accomplishment'.

These fundamental differences are reflected in the way men and women communicate with each other, says Gray. When a man has a problem he retreats into his 'cave' to try and work out a solution, whereas when a woman has a problem she wants to talk about it. The book is peppered with examples of 'translations' between Martian and Venusian – how to interpret the communications of the opposite sex. Thus, says Gray, when a woman asks a man, 'What's the matter?' and he responds, 'I am OK', it is an abbreviated version of what he really means, which is 'I am OK because I can deal with this alone. I do not need any help. Please support me by not worrying about me. Trust that I can deal with it all by myself'. Without this translation, says Gray, women misinterpret '"I am OK". It sounds to her as if he is denying his feelings or problems. She then attempts to help him by asking questions or talking about what she thinks the problem is. She does not know that he is speaking an abbreviated language'.

Some psychologists attribute these differences to underlying variations in the ways male and female brains are hardwired. Others believe it is all to do with early programming that encourages men to hide their feelings and women to express them. Yet others say it is a result of little boys having to break away psychologically from their mothers. Whatever the truth of the matter, common sense – and the sales figures of all the thousands of self-help relationship books – suggests that there are real differences in the way men and women communicate and that the gender war is not going to go away.

US psychologists Gottman and Levenson offer an intriguing hypothesis to explain men's tendency to retreat into their caves.[20] Focusing on the difference between the way married couples interact, they reviewed a large number of studies suggesting that men's autonomic nervous system – things like pace of heartbeat, level of blood pressure, speed of breathing – is more easily aroused by stress. When couples are at odds, the men concerned are able to deal with a low level of conflict. However, when there is a high level of conflict men tend to withdraw because they become physiologically aroused and seek to calm themselves in this way. A possible reason for this is that the natural consummation for male anger is physical attack – which is inappropriate in the marital context.

In earlier generations these differences in expression may have been more readily accepted simply because male and female roles were more rigid. Today, with fewer extended family ties, meaning that men and women are more dependent upon each other for emotional support, together with changes in expectations and the move towards an ideal of a more companionate marriage, both men and women may be looking for greater intimacy and understanding than they were in the past.

# 7

# Making it last

*Most women marry hoping their husband will change, and he doesn't.*
*Most men marry hoping their wife won't change, and she does.*

Anon.

If we were to judge the likely success of romantic love from the lyrics of popular songs and operas and the language of poetry, we would have to assume that most love affairs end in tears and a broken heart for one (or both) of the participants. Against this, we would need to balance the optimism of romantic literature – everything from Mills & Boon to Jane Austen and the fairy stories where the heroine finds her prince and they live happily ever after. Yet in real life, we know only too well that neither of these models offers a complete or accurate portrait of the way we experience love – it is rarely that tragic or that idyllic. Relationships usually have their ups and downs, but many do survive despite quite serious difficulties and the partners stay together more or less happily. Nevertheless, most people have experienced the emotional trauma of the slow death or sudden ending of a relationship, which can disrupt their happiness and ability to get on with their lives for weeks, months or even years.

Statistics show that in the UK, as in other western European countries and the USA, more relationships are breaking down than ever before. In 1997, there were around 180,000 divorces in Britain, compared to around 30,000 in 1961, according to the Social Trends survey reported in 2000.[1] This means that, on current trends, two in every five marriages will end in divorce. Even so, the odds on a couple staying together are better if they are married than if they are cohabiting: couples who live together are three or four times more likely to break up. According to a report from the Family Policy Studies Centre in March 2000, there are 1.6 million lone parent families, of whom single mothers are the fastest growing group. 'Twenty years ago such women would have married, only to see their relationship end in separation or divorce,' say the report's authors. 'Single lone mothers should be seen as the equivalent of teenagers in earlier generations whose shotgun marriages failed.'[2]

Despite the increase in cohabitation and the tendency for couples to delay marriage until they are older, most of us do still marry. Yet statistics from the USA show that at least half the couples who confidently promise to stay together 'till death us do part' actually end up in the divorce courts some years later, and those who marry for a second time have even less chance of staying the course.[3] As in the UK, those who opt to live together either before marriage or without ever tying the knot are even more likely to separate than those who do marry. The author of one study of modern marriage has suggested that cohabiting couples do not subscribe to conventional values to the same degree as those who choose to marry, and that it is this lack of conventionality which may account for the higher rate of relationship breakdown, rather than the fact that the couples have lived together without going through a marriage ceremony.[4]

Of the 23.6 million households in Britain, almost a third consist of a person living alone, almost three times as many as in 1961. By no means all of these 6 million people would choose to live with a partner if they could, but the Family Policy Studies Centre report paints a picture of a society that is changing and where, according to the authors, 'marriage and partnerships are more fragile than they were'.

To some extent, the increasing number of people living alone or as lone parent families can be attributed to cultural changes within society as a whole. In the 1960s, for all their reputation as an era of sexual freedom, single motherhood and divorce were still stigmatised and few women could afford to leave unsatisfactory marriages, especially if they had children. Even today, it is rarely an easy option. Nevertheless, more and more people appear to be opting for the single life, in many cases because it seems preferable to an unhappy relationship or because they have not yet found anyone with whom they would want to live.

## Healthy arguments

So what factors determine whether couples will bail out at the first hint of trouble or will one day be photographed happily cutting their golden anniversary cake? Research suggests that neither material comfort nor compatibility is as critical as romantic novelists would have us believe – although both undoubtedly help. The crucial factor as far as a happy and long-lasting marriage is concerned seems to be the way the couple handles conflict. Those people who do their best to avoid arguments at all costs and those who keep picking away at an argument are most likely to find their relationship heading for the rocks, it would seem. Men are particularly prone to avoidance tactics, while women tend to harp on a disagreement and even deliberately inflame the situation. A study by Howard Markman, which followed 135 couples over 12 years, found that 21 of them separated or divorced during that period.[5] Couples' inability to handle conflict was a strong indicator of relationship breakdown. The men in failing marriages were more likely to deny conflicts or withdraw and refuse to deal with them, while women were more likely to exaggerate conflicts or push their partners to the point where they ended up engaging in a swingeing war of words. In fact the researchers were able to predict in an astonishing 93 per cent of cases which couples were heading for breakdown simply by studying whether they dealt with disagreements in a healthy or unhealthy way. It seems that if the normal disagreements that all couples have aren't handled in a satisfactory way resentment starts to build up. This fuels destructive patterns of behaviour and eventually negative feelings begin to outweigh the positive ones and destroy the marriage.

In later work, Howard Markman further details tactics couples use when arguing. He found that marriages were most likely to break down when the individuals concerned preferred either to walk away from arguments or to let small disagreements fester until they became a serious focus of conflict. He identified several approaches that were particularly inflammatory.[6] The first is a tactic he dubs 'Beam me up Scotty' or the 'appeal to God', in which the husband, tired of his wife's incessant nagging, rolls his eyes heavenward as if in search of divine intervention. This, he found, was virtually guaranteed to fan the flames rather than cool the conflict. Another risky tactic is to terminate an argument by saying, 'I give up. Have it your own way. Just say what you want and I'll do it'. As Markman comments, 'We know from Neville Chamberlain and Hitler that appeasement doesn't work. It's like saying, "You take Poland and Czechoslovakia but just leave us alone"'. The result is invariably escalation as the frustrated spouse expresses her anger at not being heard and uses ever more powerful weapons in the hope of triggering a response. Another sign that breakdown is likely is when a relatively minor disagreement is allowed to snowball until it becomes much more serious. As Markman puts it, 'You start off disagreeing about how to put the soap in the dishwasher and wind up talking about leaving'. The most dangerous tactic of all, according to Markman, is character assassination; an acid gibe, such as 'You should get a brain transplant', may only be erased by a great many acts of kindness.

Other psychologists have suggested how a negative spiral can become entrenched within a relationship.[7] By way of illustration, they cite the example of a wife constantly nagging her partner to pick up his socks and put them in the linen basket. If he eventually does so the nagging is reinforced and so is likely to become a regular feature of her behaviour. Concessions to the will of the partner are a good thing but only if made in an open and upfront way, preferably involving trade-offs from the other. If they arise out of a unilateral collapse under pressure, then festering resentment is likely to result.

## Soft looks and honeyed words

John Gottman of Washington University has made an extensive study over the last two decades of the differences between happy and unhappy marriages. One of the most revealing was an eight-year study of 130 newlyweds, during the course of which couples filled in questionnaires, were interviewed by researchers and were videotaped to see how they resolved conflict, settled disagreements, handled fights and gave or took advice.[8] Intriguingly, the researchers found that the traditional advice of marriage counsellors to work at active listening – repeating back what the other person has said using such phrases as, 'So what you are really saying is...' – didn't work. They surmise that asking couples to use such techniques in the middle of heated argument is completely unrealistic and requires more self-control than most people possess.

What the researchers did find was that in unhappy marriages husbands tended to be autocratic, failed to listen to their wives' grievances and were contemptuous when they offered advice. Wives in unhappy marriages tended to voice complaints and advice in aggressive, confrontational ways that sparked an angry riposte from their husbands. Gottman also found that unhappy couples shared too few positive experiences.[9] He was able to predict which of 2,000 couples would end up parting by working out a simple equation: happy couples have at least five times as many positive as negative experiences; unhappy couples have about the same number of positive and negative experiences. In happy marriages, by contrast, husbands listened and either accepted advice or conceded that there was value in it even if they didn't agree on every detail. Wives in these marriages took care to express grievances and advice in gentle, soothing ways, which their husbands found easier to tolerate.

Nothing too surprising in that really, but it seems that many couples can't get it right. Speaking in interviews with *The Times*[10] and the *Los Angeles* Times,[11] Gottman likens a successful marriage to a jazz quartet. 'It's about the music a couple makes together... and the way they improvise.' Arguing, he says, 'can be one of the healthiest things a couple can do', provided they make up easily and are as free with affection as with anger. From his observations, he concludes that the best tips to enable a couple to enjoy a happy marriage are: 'To improve the quality of friendship between a husband and wife and to help them deal with disagreements differently. There has to be a kind of gentleness in the way conflict is managed. Men have to be more accepting of a woman's position and women have to be more gentle in starting up discussions'.

Peter Fraenkel and colleagues outline a preventive approach to helping couples in marital difficulty.[12] They argue that too many couples seek help too late, after irreversible damage to the relationship has occurred. If problems are addressed in the early stages, couples can be taught attitudes and skills for reducing conflict. One interesting technique is to use an egg timer to ensure that each partner is guaranteed two minutes to have their say in an argument without interruption from the other.

## Transitional stresses

It is well-known that changes in one's life pattern are stressful, hence psychologists have looked at the effects that life's transitions – events such as getting married, the birth of a child and losing an existing job or starting a new one – have on a couple's relationship.

Getting married is itself the first major transition and – contrary to romantic myth – research suggests that the hearts and roses phase of marriage lasts barely as long as the icing on the wedding cake. Studying 100 newlyweds, US psychologist Ted Huston and his colleagues found that within 3 to 15 months of walking down the aisle several key aspects of their relationship took a dive.[13] Couples reported themselves less satisfied with their marriage and their sex lives, they declared their love for each other less often, complimented each other less and disclosed their feelings less often. What is more, although they spent only a little less time with each other than before getting married, more of this shared time was dedicated to tasks like shopping, cleaning the house and so on and less to talking to each other, going out and having fun than in the courtship phase. Despite this deterioration, Huston reported that most couples were still more happy than unhappy with their relationships.

As Carol Sigelman and David Shaffer observe, 'Blissfully happy relationships evolve into still happy but more ambivalent ones'.[14] Is this because we blind ourselves to our partner's faults in the blissful days before we tie the knot or gloss over them in the hope that they will change? Or is it because we start to take each other for granted and no longer make as much of an effort once we've hooked a matc? Nobody knows. However, one thing that is abundantly clear is that marriage is not a static entity but a constantly evolving relationship that goes through many changes right from the start.

Another important point of transition is the birth of a child.

Although most new parents say that the arrival of a baby improves their lives as a whole,[15] their satisfaction with each other plummets after the birth of a first child. Perhaps not surprisingly this is more marked for women than for men.[16, 17] In reality, a baby's arrival generally has more of an impact on the mother than it does on the father, even in these days of shared parenting. The marriage takes another downturn after the birth of subsequent children and only begins to improve when the children leave home (see Figure 7.1).

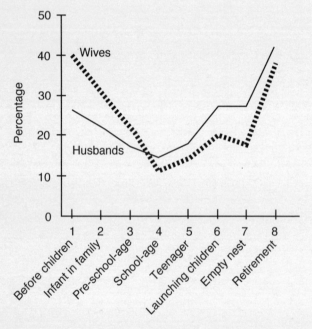

Figure 7.1 How major events in the life cycle of a marriage influence the percentage of wives and husbands who say their marriage is going well 'all the time' (from Rollins and Feldman, 1970[18])

The reasons why the arrival of a child reduces marital happiness are complex but have much to do with the creation of triangular relationships. As the wife begins to devote much of her time and attention to the newcomer, the husband is apt to feel left out. This, together with any period of enforced sexual abstinence during and after the pregnancy, might increase the chance that he will seek solace in an affair. Certainly, there is a decline in the frequency of intercourse during the first pregnancy.[19] The increased strain on family finances and curtailment of social activities also need to be considered. Finally, there is the possibility that the arrival of children does not so much cause marital unhappiness as make it more difficult for an unhappy couple to part company.

Some couples and individuals within couples seem to be better than others at coping with the stress of having a child.[20] This may depend on their degree of resilience, which in turn may depend on their childhood experiences. Additionally, research has found that older parents who conceive after marriage and who delay having children tend to adapt better than young people who have a child shortly after marriage, as they are having to adjust to being married at the same time as getting used to having a baby.[21] Couples who have realistic expectations of how a new baby is likely to change their lives tend to find this adjustment easier than those who see having a baby through rose-coloured spectacles.[22] The same is true of couples who remember their own parents as being warm and accepting and those who have good support from their partners, friends and/or relatives.

## Great expectations

It is asking a lot to expect everyone to love their partner until death as earlier generations did, because of the greatly increased life expectancy of couples who marry today. In Victorian times, marriages were frequently ended prematurely by death – often as a result of women dying in childbirth – rather than by divorce. And despite politicians' agendas, the happy, unbroken, nuclear family is becoming more and more rare as a greater percentage of the population than ever before now lives in single adult households. Serial relationships are increasingly replacing lifelong partnerships.

Sociologists Kathleen Kiernan and Ganka Mueller analysed three major surveys of adult lives.[23] They identified several groups who are divorce-prone: those who are deprived, those who have lived with a partner more than once before marriage, those who embarked on a relationship at a very young age, those whose parents divorced and those who have low emotional wellbeing. This last group encompasses people who are depressed, lacking in self-esteem or who otherwise feel bad about themselves. In other words, quite a lot of us are at risk.

It should not be thought that divorce is necessarily a pathological phenomenon, however, for others have noted that eminent and creative people (such as many of those listed in *Who's Who*) also have a higher than average divorce rate. This may have something to do with their 'resale value' – the ease with which new relationships can be formed. Thus divorce is by no means the preserve of people who are failures in life.

Problems such as boredom, disagreements and disillusionment are probably inevitable from time to time in any relationship, especially given that the ideal of modern marriage demands that partners spend so much time together and expect so much from each other. And with the decline of Christianity and traditional morals, infidelity and affairs are not as socially unacceptable as they once were – although they always existed. However, it may be that infidelity is now more destructive of relationships because people expect their partners to behave perfectly. As Penny Mansfield, director of the marriage and partnership research charity One Plus One, was reported as saying in *The Guardian*, 'The enemy of the long-term relationship is this desire for perfection. The idea that as soon as the partnership doesn't feel right, it must be intrinsically wrong'.[24]

One Plus One conducted its own research to see what makes for a long-lasting relationship. Subjects cited companionship, shared hopes and ideals, mutual respect and, most importantly, the capacity to weather the bad times.[25] These findings echo earlier research carried out by US psychologists Benjamin Karney and Thomas Bradbury.[26] In a wide-ranging review of different psychological approaches to marriage research they conclude, 'Married couples must adapt to a variety of stressful events and circumstances that they encounter over the course of their lives. The capacity of a couple to adapt depends on the degree of stress they experience and the enduring vulnerabilities that each spouse brings to the marriage. Couples' accumulated experiences with adaptive processes gradually influence their perceptions of their marital quality, which ultimately contribute to the stability of the marriage'.

Finally, it seems to help if one can somehow contrive to idealise the partner – to retain the rose-coloured spectacles for as long as possible. In a series of studies by Sandra Murray and colleagues it was found that couples who were able to see their imperfect partners in a charitable light (that is, see attributes in them that they did not even claim for themselves) were able to construct healthy relationships.[27] Their satisfaction increased progressively and conflicts were reduced over time. Murray *et al* note that positive illusions concerning the partner are self-fulfilling, such that, in their words, 'Love is not blind, but prescient'. In marriage, as in other aspects of life, it helps 'to look for the silver lining'.

# 8

# Putting it about

*The prerequisite to a good marriage is the licence to be unfaithful.*
Carl Jung[1]

Most people have heard stories of idyllic (usually tropical) island societies where there are no restrictions on sexual activity, but the reality is that such freedom is rare, if indeed it exists anywhere. Most cultures attempt to control who may have sex with whom and in what circumstances. In practice, this may mean that a man is permitted to have multiple partners, though a woman is not, although Western society has traditionally paid lip service at least to the principle of monogamy. The idea that women should be free to have multiple partners as and when they like has been anathema in most societies and is acceptable in relatively few countries even today.

One assumption that might explain this level of control is that the sex drive of human beings is so powerful that it cannot be allowed full rein or chaos would ensue. The problem here would be to explain why this would apply to women more than men. One would have to presume that power was patriarchal and men were seeking to repress female sexuality. Yet female elders seem equally intent on monitoring the morality of young women, and so one is left to conclude that the double standard emerges because the consequences of sex for women (possible pregnancy) are far more serious than those for men.

In some Western countries at least, the social pressure to conform to these norms has been decreasing in recent years, and there is a more permissive attitude towards female sexuality, although there are still many different views on what comprises acceptable sexual conduct. So what do we really know about human sexual behaviour and preferences and do men and woman differ in these areas?

Some researchers have looked for clues in the behaviour of animals. Studies suggest that only a tiny minority of species are monogamous – probably around 3 per cent. Mostly these are birds, but there are also some mammals and even one primate, the gibbon. However, this does not really tell us a great deal about the way humans can be expected to behave because it makes no allowance for the one ability that makes us unique within the animal kingdom – our capacity for making choices based on rational thought. People have the ability to control their behaviour if they choose to do so on the basis of any number of considerations; none of us is a slave to our biological urges. It is important to bear this in mind when considering some of the scientific contributions in this field. Even if we accept that evolution has programmed us through our genes to have inbuilt drives – for eating, sex or aggression, for example – we are nevertheless free agents in that we can opt not to follow these instincts if we wish to do so.

Another significant difference between humans and most other animals is that we are able – and frequently willing – to have sex at any time, not only when the female is in a fertile phase. In practice, women may feel more inclined to have sex at certain times in their menstrual cycle – particularly around the time of ovulation in many cases – which clearly has a reproductive advantage. It is also the case that men find them more attractive in the fertile phases. Some biologists think that this constant readiness for sex has evolved so as to strengthen and enhance the bonds between a couple and so keep them together

Putting it About

for long enough to raise their offspring. Others think that the 'permanent heat' of human females is better described as 'disguised ovulation', that is, a permanent 'coolness' that gives her better control over her sexual favours.[2] The survival value of such a strategy is apparent. In this way, sex could be effectively traded for resources.

## Are men polygamous?

There are good reasons for assuming that men have a natural tendency to seek variety in their partners. The majority of primates – our nearest animal relatives – opt for polygyny (one male having several female consorts at the same time). It has been, and still is in some parts of the world, a common set-up among humans too, and even in those societies that outwardly disapprove of such arrangements, it has often been considered normal for men to have mistresses as well as wives (see Figure 8.1). The evolutionary explanation for the prevalence of polygyny assumes that it is based on men's biologically driven urge to spread their seed (and thus their genes) as widely as possible. The more children a man has, the more likely he is to have some that survive to reproduce in their turn. The pioneer sexologist A C Kinsey, writing as far back as 1948, said that 'the human male would be promiscuous throughout the whole of his life if there were no social restrictions',[3] which, while it may be a rather sweeping generalisation, probably contains an element of truth.

Some researchers have ascribed this tendency to an inherent search for novelty; curiosity about new experiences is clearly an important feature of the make-up of many humans and it seems to be more true for men than for women. A story about US President Calvin Coolidge provides a classic illustration of this male taste for promiscuity. It is said that the first lady, while on a visit to a chicken farm with her husband, enquired how often the rooster had sex with his hens. When told that this happened around a dozen times a day, she asked her informant to pass this fact on to the President. Initially looking dismayed, he then enquired whether the rooster always favoured the same hen and was told that the opposite was in fact the case: 'He chooses a different hen every time'. The President smiled. 'Tell that to Mrs Coolidge', he said. Thus the tendency for male animals to be reinvigorated by novel partners has become known as 'the Coolidge effect'.

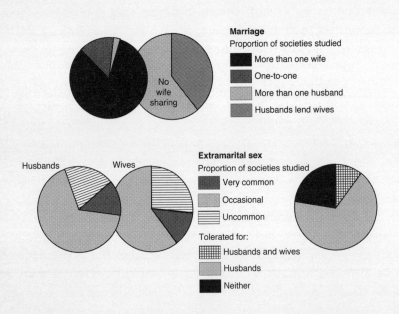

Figure 8.1 Marriage arrangements and attitudes towards extramarital sex in societies around the world. Polygyny is common, whereas polyandry is almost unknown, and affairs are better tolerated for men than women (from Campbell, 1989[4])

## Are women monogamous?

In evolutionary terms men have everything to gain and little to lose from promiscuity. However, promiscuous sex is a lot more risky for women because of the burden of childrearing. According to this theory, a woman has evolved to be choosy because she wants the fittest sire for her offspring and because she could not afford to become pregnant without a man to support and provide for her and her child. This makes it impractical for her to have multiple partners (polyandry), none of whom might be prepared to take on the responsibilities of fatherhood, and militates against adultery in case her 'permanent' partner abandoned her. In many Western societies, this restriction no longer holds true for many women. They have the option of contraception or, in many cases, of bringing up a child without the support of a long-term male partner. But, of course, such changes have not had sufficient time to affect genes, instincts and emotions.

Some psychologists have gone further and theorised that women prefer things this way because they have evolved to have a greater need for security and love than their male partners.[5] According to this view, women are genetically programmed to look for love and a secure, long-term relationship, while men are programmed to place sex at the top of their list of priorities. This may be true as a generalisation, but in reality the situation is a lot more complicated than that.

Irrespective of theories about possible differences between men and women with regard to their willingness to have sex with someone other than their regular partner, the fact is that some women have always had sexual affairs outside marriage. The fact that pregnancy often resulted from such relationships seemed to be confirmed by a study performed by Dr E E Phillip in 1973.[6] His research involved taking blood samples from a group of men and women and their children in one ordinary town in the south-east of England. Much to his surprise, his findings revealed that as many as one in three children could not possibly have been the offspring of their official fathers. Others have since doubted whether this was a representative finding, and have suggested that a figure of between 1 in 10 and 1 in 20 is more believable. Statistics kept by the Child Support Agency and based on tests conducted when fathers being pursued for maintenance denied paternity suggest that 10 per cent is the likely average. Even this figure, which takes no account of those women whose affairs did not result in pregnancy, contradicts the assumptions generally made about women's supposed preference for monogamy.

There is some evidence that the number of children whose genetic father is not the same as their acknowledged one may vary with a woman's social class. Two studies conducted in the 1990s in two tower block communities in different parts of England found figures as high as 30 per cent. If this figure is truly typical of working-class but not middle-class families, it might simply mean that women in more comfortable circumstances have more to lose if they alienate the family 'provider' by having sex with other men. It does not necessarily say anything about their desire (or lack of it) for multiple partners, or their standards of behaviour. (For a discussion of such issues, see Baker and Oram.[7])

## Men and their genes

In his influential and controversial book *The Selfish Gene*,[8] ethologist Richard Dawkins discusses why males and females of different species might adopt different strategies in terms of a preference for single or multiple sexual partners so as to maximise their chances of passing on their genes successfully. Pointing out that both monogamy and polygyny are common social structures in human societies, he suggests that 'man's way of life is largely determined by culture rather than genes'; an idea that might surprise many who have only a general idea of his work. 'However,' he goes on, 'it is still possible that human males in general have a tendency towards promiscuity, and females a tendency towards monogamy, as we would predict on evolutionary grounds. Which of these two tendencies wins in particular societies depends on details of cultural circumstances, just as in different animal species it depends on ecological details'.

Whether or not they agree that transmission of genes is of prime significance as far as the reproductive urge is concerned, virtually no one would question that having and raising children who can then themselves reproduce is vital from an evolutionary perspective. As far as the male is concerned, he could adopt one of two strategies to increase his chances of successfully achieving this objective. He might aim to impregnate as many women as possible in the hope that at least some of the resulting children would survive. Alternatively, he could invest all his energies in a single partner, staying around to ensure that no other male is able to gain access and father children with her. Both these approaches are used in other species and both offer a reasonable prospect of success. One expert has suggested that biology may play a part in determining which option an individual male decides to go for. Those who choose the multiple partner approach may be the ones with a very high sex drive, suggests zoologist Robin Baker.[9] According to Baker's research, a male's desire to have frequent sex may be predicted by the size of his testicles, large ones being linked with a high sex drive. Baker points out that testicle size as well as high libido is genetically determined.

Scientists have looked to our nearest relatives in the animal world – especially gorillas and chimpanzees – for clues to the possible relationships between sexual behaviour and physical features such as genital size. Male gorillas have a harem of females and use their massive size and strength to defend them against other males. Thus they do not need large testicles to produce large quantities of sperm that can compete with the sperm of rival males. Chimpanzees are promiscuous, though a male may have a short 'honeymoon' period with one female before moving on to fresh pastures. This means that they need to ensure that they produce sufficient sperm to 'overpower' that of any other males who may have had sex with the same female. This is why they have larger testicles than gorillas, relative to their body size. In both these instances, the females appear to copulate willingly, but the same is not true of orang-utans: the males effectively rape the females, overpowering them by physical force. At the other extreme are gibbons, where males and females bond for life and, significantly, there is no difference in size between them. When these criteria are used to assess humans, they fall somewhere in the middle. Men are, on average, slightly larger than women, and their testicles are neither excessively small nor excessively large in relation to body size (see Figure 8.2). This ties in with the observable patterns of human male sexual behaviour – they may opt for polygyny (like gorillas), promiscuity (like chimpanzees), lifelong pair bonding (like gibbons) or even, on occasion, for rape (like orang-utans). All of these strategies are capable of promoting gene survival.

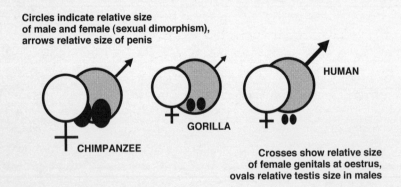

Figure 8.2 Relative size of body and genitals in three types of great ape (from Short, 1979[10])

An interesting thing apparent in this diagram is that the human male has a very large penis relative to the other great apes. The reason for this is not known, though some have speculated that female preferences operating over thousands of years may be responsible, men with larger penises being more likely to perpetuate their genes (the peacock's enormous tail is similarly thought to have evolved as a result of female choice). In other apes the females do not enjoy orgasm – the male performance is too quick. Human females may have selected mates with large penises because they had a better chance of reaching orgasm with them. Orgasm is not only rewarding but is believed to increase fertility and the desire to bond with a mate.

## Who needs more sex?

Some recent work raises the possibility that genes may play a hitherto unsuspected role in determining whether a person has a tendency to sexual promiscuity. 'How often you want to have sex may well be determined in your genes,' says Dean Hamer, a molecular geneticist at the National Institutes of Health in Bethesda, Maryland. He and his fellow researchers studied a group of 250 men and found that half of them had what the team call a 'high libido gene'. These men were more likely than those without this specific gene to have frequent sex – once a day or more. Those who did not have this gene were satisfied with a much less active sex life, some being content to have sex no more than three times a year. The gene appears to work through its ability to modulate brain levels of a neurotransmitter called serotonin, which is involved in the control of the sex drive. High levels provide a feeling of satisfaction with one's lot – so that sexual thrills are less sought-after.[11]

Since low serotonin is also a characteristic of people suffering from depression, it is interesting to speculate whether some highly sexually active men might pursue sex as an antidote to depression. High-profile men alleged to be 'sex addicts', such as actors Michael Douglas and David Duchovny, have both been reported as wishing to change their behaviour, recognising that it can be self-destructive. Commenting on the question of whether such chronic promiscuity can genuinely be defined as an addiction in strict psychiatric terms, psychologist Oliver James has suggested that such people 'get nearly all the same things from sex that drug addicts get from drugs and alcoholics from drink: an intensely pleasurable high, comparable to nothing else in their lives; a means to anaesthetise painful feelings such as sadness, loneliness and anger; and a way to escape the pressures and problems of daily living'.[12] He goes on to suggest that hypersexual people may be trying to compensate for a lack of emotional satisfaction and closeness, which stems from childhood experiences. In fact, says James, it is a vain quest because intimacy and emotional closeness cannot be achieved through sex alone.

While having the high libido gene might explain why some people have a need for very frequent sex, it does not necessarily imply that they must be promiscuous. Should they happen to have a regular partner with a similar libido, they may have no need or wish to seek out other people to meet their desires. Dean Hamer has suggested that the need to have a variety of sexual partners may be more widespread among people with a particular (long) form of a gene concerned with D4 (dopamine), which is a chemical messenger in the brain. In 1998, he reported that males with this form of the gene were not content with a single sexual partner and were more likely to try to have sex with a variety of women than those who had a different form. Hamer, then, finds two different libido genes – one concerned with sexual frequency and the other with promiscuity.

Naturally, this work does not lack critics. The doubts about its validity centre around the widely accepted view that a single gene cannot determine behaviour in such a straightforward way. Most experts in the field believe that while genes may have some bearing on the way a person behaves, other factors such as upbringing, emotional experiences, personal morality and cultural norms are equally important. The same criticism has been directed at reports of genetic research pointing to the existence of genes that predispose people to violent or criminal behaviour or to homosexuality. Claiming that you can't help behaving the way you do because your genes are 'making' you do it may be a convenient get-out but it doesn't absolve you of responsibility for your actions. Nevertheless, such discoveries do suggest that genetic inheritance plays a more significant role in influencing the way we turn out than we might think; nature is reclaiming some territory that was previously thought to belong exclusively to nurture.

## 'Chemical' fidelity

An animal research project at Emory University in the USA in 1999 provides food for thought on the subject of monogamy. The work focused on the prairie vole, a creature that remains totally faithful to its first sexual partner, normally opting to remain celibate if its partner dies. The team used genetic engineering techniques to insert prairie vole genes into a mouse, which does not pair for life in this way, and succeeded in turning it into a model of marital fidelity. Team leader Thomas Insel was quoted as saying: 'The results so far suggest love is simply a form of addiction that makes some animals form these lifelong pair bonds'.[13] He ascribes this to the influence of two hormones – oxytocin and vasopressin – which affect social behaviour and memory formation respectively. The release of these chemicals during the initial encounter is responsible, Insel believes, for creating the bond between mating voles through the effect they have on areas of the brain linked with addiction. The team demonstrated the effects of these hormones by manipulating their levels so as to cause the voles to form a pair bond even though they had not had sex and by inhibiting the bonding effect even though the animals had mated.

While it is known that oxytocin and vasopressin are involved in creating the sense of closeness and euphoria that humans experience in a love relationship, it would seem that their effect on us is not as powerful – or perhaps just not as long-lasting – as it is in Insel's rodents. Many people still seek out variety in their sexual partners or would like to do so if they could. And of course, human relationships are influenced by many factors other than hormones.

## Women's ways

The traditional theories about how a woman goes about choosing a mate and, more specifically, a father for her children, have concentrated on her need to find a man who has both 'good quality' genes and the potential to be a good provider. Genetic quality is indicated by such things as health, good looks, intelligence and athletic prowess. Assessing his potential as a provider is more difficult, but ideally he needs to be wealthy, generous and reliable. In the past at least, this has often meant that he will be older and therefore more materially successful than the woman herself. These requirements are often not easily met by a single person. In addition, a good-looking, fit and successful man is likely to have his choice of partners and it may not be easy to get him to commit himself, particularly to a woman who is not perceived as highly desirable, for whatever reason. Such male paragons are not that widely available anyway, and many women are left with no choice but to settle for a compromise. One way of getting round this dilemma was discussed on page 128, when we looked at the numbers of children who are not in fact genetically related to their acknowledged fathers. It could be that some of these mothers have tried to beat the odds by selecting a genetically well-endowed man as the father of their child while choosing a less impressive specimen as their long-term partner because of his potential as a provider.

According to Baker, women may in fact increase their chances of reproducing if they have affairs.[14] As well as gaining the opportunity to have sex with a man who is appealing because he seems a good bet genetically, a woman may be enhancing her chances of conception at the same time. Baker presents evidence that a woman is more likely to have an orgasm with such a man and this increases her chances of retaining his sperm. His research showed that when a woman has an orgasm, the entrance to her cervix dips down into the top of her vagina where a pool of semen will collect after her partner has ejaculated, so sucking more of it up into her uterus.[15] Thus the ideal scenario is for her to reach a climax at the same time or immediately after the man, a sequence of events that is apparently more likely to occur with a lover than with a regular partner. If it should happen that she has intercourse with both her lover and her partner within a single week, it is possible that both lots of sperm will be capable of fertilising her ovum. Which one actually manages to do so, says Baker, depends on which is most capable of winning the race to penetrate the ovum. The victor in this 'sperm war' may win because it is the 'fittest' in evolutionary terms, so by triggering this war the woman ensures the best genetic inheritance for her child.

Other research has backed the idea that the female orgasm may actually increase the likelihood of conception. A group of biologists at the University of Cardiff reported in 1998 that when a woman found sex pleasurable and satisfying, she retained more of her partner's sperm.[16] The team asked 103 women in their mid-thirties to rate their last sexual encounter in terms of the degree of satisfaction they had derived from it. They were then given a post-coital test within three hours of having had sex. Of those women who gave the experience a low score, nearly half had a post-coital count of zero, showing that they had not retained any sperm. In contrast, among the high scorers, only 1 in 10 had a low post-coital test result. The team speculated that the vaginal spasms that occur when a woman has an orgasm might help to propel sperm into the uterus, so improving the chances of her conceiving. Additionally, it might be that high levels of arousal create a more sperm-friendly environment in the vagina and the cervix by lowering acidity levels. It should not be imagined, however, that orgasm is necessary for conception. The great apes, and many women, seldom experience orgasm but still manage to get pregnant.

## An eternal triangle

An intriguing new light is shed upon the way women might balance the relative advantages of monogamy and infidelity by the authors of a 1998 report entitled 'The logic of *ménage à trois*'. Evolutionary biologists at the University of Stockholm devised a mathematical game involving three characters: a heterosexual couple who live together and a male lover who pops up from time to time.[17] The game was set up to allow the two main players a number of options, which each carried rewards and penalties. If the male member of the couple chose to have affairs, he might then be rewarded with a number of children but he would also risk his wife having sex with the lover. If he chose to stay around and fend off the attentions of the lover, he might have more children with his partner and would be in no doubt as to their parentage. The woman faced similar choices. She could remain faithful to her partner, have many children with him and hope to encourage him to stay and help her bring them up. However, if he did stray, she could avail herself of the chance to have children with the lover.

The team found that the game usually produced one of two outcomes: in one the couple remained mutually faithful and the lover eventually disappeared, without having fathered children with the woman. Thus he lost out from a genetic point of view. Alternatively, the male member of the couple chose to have affairs, so hopefully spreading his genes among many offspring, while the female flirted with the lover – the *ménage à trois*. The researchers suggested that the female could use this flirtatious behaviour to discourage her partner from having affairs, but for such a tactic to be credible there must be a real possibility that she would actually have sex with the lover.

The authors claim that this kind of social set-up might account for recognised anomalies of parentage – at least in non-human species. For example, studies of supposedly monogamous birds have found that as many as one in five offspring of a given pair is not genetically related to the male bird (he, it seems, has been 'cuckooed'). And, as we have seen, such instances are not unknown among humans either! Applying their results to the animal kingdom, the authors conclude that where male birds are faithful, flirtatious behaviour by the female contributes to keeping them so.

There is accumulating evidence that, in non-human species at least, females may have much to gain from a reproductive point of view by having multiple sex partners. One study has shown that when hens are inseminated they may choose to reject the cock's sperm – ejecting it from their bodies immediately after copulation has occurred.[18] The author suggests that females of other species make similar 'choices'; there is evidence, he believes, that human females may spontaneously abort very early embryos (when they consist of just a small number of cells) if they are not satisfactory.

Support for the argument that women as well as men may be genetically inclined towards infidelity is provided by anthropologist Helen Fisher, of Rutgers University near New York. She has suggested that women may be ready to look for a new partner within a relatively short time of marrying or moving in with a man.[19] The reason is that she is genetically 'programmed' to try to ensure the best possible survival chances for her children, and the best way to do this is to have them with a variety of different fathers who will pass on different strengths and abilities. According to Fisher, four years may be the time span allocated by nature to each relationship. This is because the chemistry that creates the sensation of being in love changes and stops being effective after about 36 months, although it may well take another 12 months before the woman becomes completely aware that she is no longer in love with her partner. Social changes that are making it increasingly possible for women to change partners when they choose – or even to live apart from their children's father – mean that more women will follow the dictates of their genes and move on, she says. Nevertheless, she does not suggest that all or even the majority of relationships will end this way. Many couples develop close bonds of affection that make them want to stay together even though the first heady rush of passion has disappeared.

Heidi Greiling and David Buss studied the particular contexts in which women would be unfaithful to their partner and what, specifically, they sought to gain by doing so.[20] Testing a variety of different hypotheses about the potential benefits of extramarital relations, they found solid support for two in particular:

1.  the *mate-switching* hypothesis – trying to find a replacement for the current partner who would be better in some respects; and

2.  *resource acquisition* – obtaining some immediate material gain.

Less support was found for the other theories, such as seeking genetically diverse offspring and manipulating the current partner (for example, paying them back for past infidelity or deterring them from such behaviour in the future).

## Who plays away?

There has been a considerable amount of research in recent years devoted to identifying which individuals are particularly likely to have affairs outside marriage or long-term relationships. One study of 136 male and 169 female US college students looked at the factors associated with the tendency to have multiple sexual partners.[21] Those preferring a ludic love style within Lee's classification[22] were the ones who had had the greatest number of sexual partners. The more closely they fitted into this category, the greater the number of partners. This held true even when the individuals concerned were involved in a close romantic relationship, and applied equally to the men and women who were studied.

A similar study of American college students looked at a wide range of behaviour; not just sex but also dating, kissing and petting with someone other than their regular partner.[23] The researchers looked for associations between particular beliefs and love styles and liaisons with other people. Although the general attitude among the students, both male and female, was disapproving of such behaviour, the majority of the 299 men and 392 women said they had in fact strayed to a greater or lesser degree while involved in a relationship. There was no difference in the amount of dating and kissing indulged in by men and women, but men were more likely to have gone in for fondling, oral sex and actual intercourse. Those who were

most likely to have had other dates or sexual experience with people not their partners were found to believe less strongly that love and sex should be confined to marriage, to have a taste for new sexual sensation and a preference for the ludic love style. They were also more convinced of their ability to lie successfully to their partners!

Different criteria were used in a study of students that attempted to predict which individuals were most likely to be unfaithful to their partners.[24] They found that the degree to which couples were committed to one another at the beginning of the academic term was a good indicator of whether they would become emotionally or physically involved with someone else at a later stage. Commitment was defined in terms of higher satisfaction, a greater degree of investment in the relationship and a lack of perceived alternatives.

Certain personality traits predispose a person to infidelity, according to researchers at the University of Texas.[25] Their study looked specifically at couples who had been married for no more than a year, and their findings were based on interviews with both partners. The researchers talked to 107 couples and found that those who were high in narcissism and psychoticism and low on conscientiousness were most susceptible to infidelity. (Narcissism refers to self-absorption; psychoticism in this context means a tendency to be aloof and lacking in concern for the feelings of others. Conscientiousness refers to reliability and social responsibility.) Narcissism was a particularly accurate predictor as far as the women were concerned, while narcissistic men tended to regard their wives as flirtatious and to suspect that they might have an affair. A person who regarded their spouse as very jealous or who was dissatisfied with their sex life was also identified as a potential or actual adulterer.

The report highlighted certain ways of behaving that might

provide clues as to whether an individual was having an affair or was of the personality type most at risk. Typical behaviours included:

- turning up late to meetings or social events;
- constantly checking/admiring their appearance in mirrors;
- playing (sometimes hurtful) practical jokes;
- dominating conversations and interrupting constantly;
- leaving unnecessary lights on;
- failing to thank friends for gifts;
- getting into debt; and
- appearing unmoved by an injured animal.

It isn't difficult to identify well-known adulterers who illustrate certain aspects of this profile. Marilyn Monroe (who had an affair with actor Yves Montand while married to playwright Arthur Miller) was notoriously late for appointments and was quoted as saying, 'I've been on a calendar but never on time'. President John F Kennedy, who was reputed to use prostitutes as well as having a number of mistresses (including Marilyn Monroe) while married to Jackie, had the White House fitted out with mirrors in every room so that he could preen himself in passing. It is doubtful, however, that the spouses of either of these famous philanderers would have needed such clues to inform them of their partners' activities!

# 9

# Lovesickness

*Scratch a lover and find a foe.*

Dorothy Parker

Relationships may end with a bang or a whimper. A blazing row may be enough to drive you apart for good but, if you have been together for any length of time, it's more probable that simmering resentments, unacceptable behaviour or even just plain boredom will finally reach a peak and force one partner (or sometimes both) to acknowledge that the relationship has run its course. Passionate and romantic love are not always based on any real, deep knowledge of the other person. The chemistry of sexual attraction and shared passion is a powerful force but if and when it fades, as it almost invariably does, the relationship may be in trouble if there is nothing else to hold the two people concerned together.

There is some evidence that couples who knew each other well before they married or moved in together have a better chance of staying together. One study found that wives who had dated their husbands for less than five months before they married were the least happy, while those who had done so for two years or more were the most happy.[1] Many researchers have also reported that partnerships that began when the individuals were relatively young are also more likely to be short-lived. This is hardly surprising when you consider that inexperience of life combined with natural personal development over time may cause people to move in different directions and create gaps between them that were not there to begin with. This may become increasingly apparent as new situations reveal hitherto unrealised differences in attitude, behaviour and emotional responses between a couple who got together when both partners were relatively young. The point is well made by Donn Byrne and Sarah Murnen:

> Few of us can know beforehand how we or the one we love will respond to parenthood, economic stress, in-laws, serious illness, spending increased amounts of discretionary income, moving, ageing, or any of the other life-changing events that are part of life. As the result of such situational changes and the new and unknown responses of each partner, extremely similar and compatible pairs can find themselves at odds about matters that neither had even considered previously.[2]

Having children can dramatically affect the balance of a relationship, however enthusiastic the couple concerned are about the prospect of becoming parents. For one thing, the woman's pregnancy and the arrival of a new baby often bring changes to a couple's sex life, even causing it to come to a complete stop for a time. (This topic is covered in more detail in Chapter 10.) How the couple deal with this and the other effects of parenthood on their way of life will have an important influence on their subsequent relationship. In one study, couples interviewed said that their activities after the arrival of a child tended to revolve more around the woman's choices, and that the man had fewer opportunities to do things on his own.[3] This does not necessarily imply that such change must have a negative effect on the relationship, but it is likely to mean that both partners must be willing and able to make the necessary adjustments.

Although having children may place stress on a relationship, difficulty having them can also create serious repercussions. In one study, researchers interviewed 107 infertile couples to assess their perception of the problems their inability to have a child created within their relationship.[4] The couples were interviewed separately, with the results showing that their self-esteem and sense of personal wellbeing were adversely affected and that the stress of infertility resulted in increased levels of conflict within the marriage. Women were more strongly affected by a loss of sexual self-esteem and satisfaction and by marital conflict; men were more influenced by the negative effects that the stress had on frequency of sexual intercourse.

## 'You've changed'

A relationship that has apparently met the needs of both partners successfully may cease to do so when circumstances change radically. For example, a man who has happily let his wife run their joint lives, looking after the home and children and planning their social life while he concentrated on his career, may be totally unable to adapt if something such as a chronic illness makes it impossible for her to continue to do this. If either or both partners begin to find that their needs are not being met, their level of commitment to the relationship may gradually decline and they become less satisfied with it.[5] A similar crisis may occur if one partner appears to change in important ways – because they enrol for further education as a mature student or take up a new and engrossing job, for example. The possible effects on a relationship were poignantly – and accurately – analysed in the play *Educating Rita*, in which a couple grow rapidly apart once Rita starts to become fascinated by the worlds of college and the intellect. The pair finally split up, although the husband continues to appear bemused by what has happened and opts to continue with his existing way of life, albeit with a new partner. In *Shirley Valentine*, another play by the same writer, Willy Russell, the heroine's husband is similarly baffled by what he sees as his wife's unreasonable behaviour when she refuses to return to her life of domesticity after her first ever experience of a Greek holiday. The idea that her actual motive is to rediscover her old self, 'the real Shirley Valentine', is difficult, if not impossible, for him to grasp. Both plays were made into highly successful films, striking a chord with many people around the world.

Although relationship difficulties may manifest themselves in a variety of ways – such as conflicts about sex, money, whether to have children and how to bring them up – the real problem may well lie at a deeper level. It is all too easy to assume that your partner wants the same things from a relationship as you do when, in fact, they have quite different ideas, which they also assume you share. For example, one partner may want to spend as much time as possible with the other, to the exclusion of family and former friends, and be reluctant to consider any kind of social activity that does not involve their 'other half'. Their partner may go along with this in the first flush of romantic passion, before they begin to feel stifled and want to make space for themselves to see old friends, resume former hobbies or just have some time alone. Or perhaps one partner feels most comfortable when life follows a smooth and relatively straight path, so that job or house moves, holidays and starting a family, for instance, are considered and planned in advance. If their partner is more of an opportunist, someone who enjoys taking risks or acting on impulse, the scene is set for real difficulties. Such problems may arise because neither has understood what the other person is really like, or because one or both, although aware of the differences between them, think that compromise will be possible. Sometimes both are prepared to give on important issues, but the gap between hope and reality simply widens and the couple draw further and further apart.

Baxter asked recently parted couples to give the main reasons why they thought their relationships had broken up.[6] The five most common reasons cited, in order of 'popularity', were:

- Desire for autonomy or problems dealing with interdependence (27% of men, 44% of women)
- Lack of similarity between the partners (27% of men, 32% of women)
- Feeling unsupported or undermined by the partner (19% of men, 33% of women)
- Lack of intimacy and openness (8% of men, 31% of women)
- Fading away of passion or romance (19% of men, 3% of women).

Clearly, the perceived problems for women are mainly to do with independence, social support and intimacy. Men also see problems in these areas, but are more concerned about lack of passion and romance.

### The boredom factor

Some of the earliest studies into the reasons for relationship breakdown confirmed what many people know from experience – the couples concerned simply become bored with one another. The fact that they can predict exactly how their partner will respond in any given situation is seen not as reassuring but as tediously predictable. In many cases, boredom extends into the bedroom, as their sex life becomes more a matter of routine than excitement or intense passion. There is growing evidence to suggest that neither men nor women are naturally monogamous and that many people have an inbuilt drive towards sexual novelty and experiment. Whether boredom is a sufficient incentive for couples to separate will depend on a variety of circumstances, practical and financial as well as personal. Sometimes they may choose to tolerate or even ignore the problem while they are bringing up their children, who at least provide a shared interest and stimulus, but be forced to face up to the aridity of their relationship once the children move away from home.

One way to offset boredom is for a couple to find new and exciting things to do together. Arthur Aron and colleagues found correlations between relationship satisfaction and the frequency of shared, 'exciting' activities a couple engaged in.[7] Taking the idea into the laboratory they were able to show that having a couple participate together in a novel and arousing task for a mere seven minutes was enough to improve the quality of their relationship (by contrast with a mundane, boring task, which offered no such gain). The authors concluded that failing to do exciting things together is a major cause of the typical decline of a relationship after the honeymoon period.

## Managing difficulties

Whatever conflicts may arise within a relationship, their precise nature may actually matter less than the way the individuals concerned choose to deal with them. To some extent, this will depend on their feelings about themselves and their partners and the way they perceive their relationship. When it comes to predicting whether partnerships will survive, one of the most significant clues is the level of commitment that the couple feels towards their relationship. If they are determined to make it last, they are likely to be prepared to tolerate their partner's bad points and make great efforts to adapt their own needs and behaviour.[8]

The attachment style (see Chapter 5) of the partners will also have a bearing on how they deal with conflict within their relationship. As you might expect, those with a secure attachment style seem most able to make the necessary adjustments, while an avoidant or anxious attachment style makes it more difficult for the person to deal positively with difficulties. One study showed that relationship counselling – often recommended to couples with problems – may actually make the situation worse for anxious and avoidant individuals.[9] The researchers asked dating couples to complete a questionnaire identifying their attachment style before discussing a problem that they regarded as significantly affecting their relationship. Anxious people found the discussion itself very stressful and said they felt less close and loving towards their partners afterwards. Although avoidant individuals were not distressed by discussing their problems, counselling made it harder for them to tackle them. The researchers noted that men with this style appeared relatively cold and lacking in support for their partners during the process. Secure individuals, by contrast, appeared to benefit from such an exchange and felt better about the relationship and about their partner afterwards.

## The role of jealousy

As Shakespeare illustrated incomparably in *Othello*, jealousy is destructive to the person experiencing it and to his or her relationship with the person on the receiving end. The majority of people who are prone to jealousy are well aware of this, yet this understanding rarely has any effect on their feelings, or on the way they behave. Like Othello, they may be responding to a perceived threat to their relationship which does not in fact exist; a lack of evidence that their partner is or is about to betray them with someone else is no bar to jealous feelings. Such people may react to the slightest 'provocation' from their lover – a conversation at a party or a phone call – and go to extreme lengths to 'prove' that their relationship is indeed threatened by their partner's behaviour. Searching pockets, handbags and briefcases, reading diaries, phoning repeatedly to check on their partner's whereabouts and questioning friends and colleagues are all common tactics that are ultimately destructive of relationships, whether or not the original jealousy was well-founded. So what drives apparently normal people to such extremes and prevents them from changing their ways, even though they may despise themselves for their underhand tactics?

Evolutionary psychologists argue that the answer lies, at least partly, in instinctive 'programming'. As far as men are concerned, one of the two possible approaches available to them to ensure the survival of their genes into the next generation is to prevent other males from impregnating their partners (the other is to spread their own genes as widely as possible). If they are not able to achieve this they may end up devoting their energies to raising the offspring of another male rather than their own (being 'cuckolded' = being 'cuckooed'). Since it may not be practical to maintain constant vigilance so as to get rid of possible rivals, jealous behaviour, which threatens the female with dire consequences should she stray sexually, might be a more effective form of defence against interlopers. The corresponding explanation as to why a woman exhibits jealous behaviour lies in her need to make the father of her children stay around to act as an effective provider until the offspring are able to survive alone. By monitoring his behaviour closely and making a big fuss any time he shows an inclination to stray, she hopes to improve the chances of his remaining faithful.

Of course, both men and women experience jealousy and, when they react emotionally to the situations that provoke it, are not consciously responding to these evolutionary imperatives. In other words, they may be unhappy or angry when they know or suspect that a partner is being unfaithful without ever giving a thought to possible implications for paternity or providing for children. Despite this, there is evidence that jealous feelings in women and men are triggered by different kinds of behaviour in ways that correspond with the hypotheses of the evolutionary psychologists. One study that demonstrates this connection was conducted by David Buss and colleagues.[10] They asked American college students to consider two questions: imagine your partner having sex with someone else, and imagine your partner falling in love with someone else. When asked to choose which of these scenarios they would find most distressing, 60 per cent of the men (compared with 17 per cent of the women) chose the first and 83 per cent of the women (but only 40 per cent of the men) chose the second.

In a second experiment, Buss's team asked 30 male and 30 female students to conjure up mental images of the two scenarios in their minds while attached to a range of devices for measuring physiological responses such as increased heart rate, sweating and frowning. The results showed that men reacted much more strongly to the images of sexual infidelity than they did to images of emotional infidelity; the women reacted the other way round, showing more signs of distress in response to emotional than to sexual infidelity. Other studies have reported similar differences between men and women in other cultures, implying that the response to different triggers is not simply a culturally influenced reaction.

Interestingly, a study of Dutch married couples in which one partner had had an affair showed that men and women tended to be more jealous depending on what they perceived as the motive for the behaviour. Men were more affected if they thought their partner was seeking sexual variety, whereas women minded more if they thought their partner was dissatisfied with them and so attracted to someone else.[11]

According to John Lee's theory of love styles (see Chapter 5), your preferred style will be a good indicator as to whether you are susceptible to jealousy and to what extent. Those who prefer Eros and Storge are likely to experience it from time to time but, as you might expect, manic lovers suffer worst of all, to the point where jealousy is an intrinsic element of their love. Equally predictably, ludic lovers rarely have jealous feelings because commitment to their lover and dependence on them for emotional security are not features of this style of love.

## Early learning

For most people, their first experiences of jealousy come not with their first adult romantic relationship, but in their childhood. Siblings are almost always jealous of one another and are frequently convinced that one or both parents love a brother or sister more. Many psychologists have suggested that this is a particular problem for first-born children, who have to learn to share the love of their parents, which was once exclusively theirs. However, a study of 100 men and 100 women in the Netherlands, conducted by Bram Buunk, found the opposite to be the case: later-born children suffered more jealousy than first-borns, a finding the author attributed to the parents lavishing more love and attention on their first child.[12] Competition for parental care and affection may have served a useful purpose in earlier centuries, where large families were the norm and the availability of emotional and physical sustenance was limited. Those who were able to ensure that their needs were met, if necessary at the expense of their siblings, were the ones most likely to make it to adulthood.

Nevertheless, carrying this constant battle for affection into adult love relationships is frequently counterproductive, tending to drive a lover away rather than encouraging him or her to remain faithful. Some people find it impossible completely to suppress the fear that their partner will stray or leave them for someone else, but they can sometimes learn to keep their jealous feelings under control. By admitting the way they feel, both to themselves and their partners, a person may come to accept that the jealous feelings have no foundation in reality and learn to live with them. Someone who understands the problem may be able to avoid unwittingly triggering these feelings and meet his or her partner's need for reassurance and support.

## Letting go

Being dumped by someone you still love happens to virtually everyone sooner or later and at the time it can seem like the end of the world. Other people invariably tell you that you'll get over it, that your lover didn't deserve you and you're better off without them, but none of that helps, even if it's true. According to one study, the more unhappy and lonely one partner feels after a relationship has broken up, the less the other is likely to share those emotions.[13] These researchers also found that women were more often the instigators of the break-up than were men, a finding confirmed not only by other studies but also by divorce statistics – more women than men instigate divorce proceedings. The reason could be that men, with their preference for polygyny, are happy to let old relationships drift while pursuing new ones, whereas women prefer serial monogamy and hence want to clean up old relationships before moving on.

In the early days and weeks following a break-up you are likely to experience a whole gamut of emotions, ranging from despair to anger, sleeplessness to loss of appetite, agitation to apathy and a total loss of self-confidence. You may blame yourself and wonder what you did wrong. You will almost certainly cry a lot and want to keep going over what happened and how you feel about it with anyone who'll listen. Harvey and colleagues found that it is very common for people to think long and hard for some time afterwards about what went wrong in an attempt to understand the cause of a relationship breaking up.[14]

Some of these painful emotional reactions can be put down to the effect on body chemistry of the sudden withdrawal of love. Some of the euphoria and excitement of love is linked to the surge of hormones and neurotransmitters triggered when you are in this state, and it takes time for your body to adjust to their disappearance. In this respect, someone who is suffering the after-effects of a relationship ending is like a recovering drug addict, as their bodies crave the chemical 'high' associated with love and drugs alike. Eventually, these withdrawal symptoms will fade and disappear and with them some of the emotional devastation.

There is probably no way of short-circuiting the recovery process; it inevitably takes time. Though you may think you'll never get over it, the truth is that you almost certainly will, eventually. In the meantime, it will relieve your feelings and help to sort out your thoughts if you are able to rely on sympathetic friends and family who are prepared to listen and offer their support and company when you need it. Generally speaking, women are more able to do this than men. They tend to have better support networks and are used to discussing emotional issues with their friends – something that many men find difficult or impossible.

In 1987, psychologist Zev Wanderer and journalist Tracy Cabot wrote a self-help book called *Letting Go*.[15] It sold itself as 'a 12-week personal action plan to overcome a broken heart' and aimed to use the techniques of behavioural psychology to teach readers to change the way they acted as the first step towards changing their underlying feelings and thoughts. This involved rewarding yourself for 'good behaviour' – such as hiding away all mementoes of your lost love and refusing to listen to your joint favourite music. 'Bad' behaviour – such as dwelling on memories of your lover – had to be punished with such unlikely devices as the smell of rotten egg. As the programme progresses, you are taken through such activities as writing a 'crime sheet' of your ex's faults and bad habits, planning a 'sob hour' at the most inconvenient time of day (when you would really rather be doing something else) and so on. By week eight, you are allowed to get out all those sad souvenirs and cry until you get bored. At the same time, you are allowed to go back to your old haunts but must do so with new people, so as to overlay the old unhappy memories with new good ones. Wanderer claimed that, despite the fact that this approach avoided any attempt at gaining insight into what went wrong in the relationship, it was effective within three months. However, not much has been heard of this approach since and its credibility was undermined for some people by the writers' personal experiences. Having begun the book as a couple, by the time it was finished they had broken up painfully and dramatically, were not speaking and would not even be interviewed together!

Although Wanderer and Cabot took the behaviourist approach to what might seem like absurd extremes, there is, nevertheless, something to be gained from the principles outlined in their book. When a relationship ends painfully, leaving one partner feeling rejected, their confidence and self-esteem take a knock, so anything that contributes to rebuilding them is worthwhile, whether that means investing in a new wardrobe or hairstyle, learning to play tennis or dance salsa or mastering a new work-related skill such as using the latest computer software. Tempting though it may be to revisit old haunts, look over photographs of the good times, play the music you enjoyed together and focus on past happiness, this tends only to keep the wound fresh and prevent you concentrating on the future. Avoiding them until you feel stronger and finding new people and activities to fill the gap left by the departed lover are more constructive. If you are able to analyse what went wrong, you may be able to gain something positive from the experience and avoid similar difficulties in a future relationship.

Of course, if your lover simply fell in love with someone else, that is not your fault but it may help to realise that it is impossible to force anyone to love you: they either do or they don't.

## Unhealthy love

The idea that love may be an addiction comparable to drugs for some women has been developed by Robin Norwood in her book *Women Who Love Too Much*. In her view, these women have a deep need for love, excitement and emotional security, which they hope to find in a romantic relationship with a man. Unfortunately, they always fall in love with what she calls 'impossible' men – those who are unstable, unreliable, immature, moody, angry, unhappy and so on – and then try to 'fix' them, an aim that is usually doomed to fail. She ascribes these women's behaviour to their early life and relationships:

> Women who love too much come from families in which they were either lonely or isolated, or rejected, or overburdened with inappropriately heavy responsibilities and so became overly nurturing and self-sacrificing; or else they were subjected to dangerous chaos so that they developed an overwhelming need to control the people around them and the situations in which they find themselves. It follows that a woman who needs to nurture, control, or both will be able to do so only with a partner who at least allows if not actually invites this kind of behaviour.[16]

Ultimately, says Norwood, women who love too much concentrate totally on trying to make the relationship work, trying to meet what they perceive as the man's needs so as to change him and make him love her. The way out of this hopeless and destructive cycle is for the woman to stop putting all her effort into the man and divert it to herself instead. She needs to become 'selfish', to stop trying to control and manipulate others and focus on her own problems and needs. To do this, she will need to gain the support of other people who understand – preferably by joining an appropriate group.

The women described by Norwood are generally only damaging themselves, but other forms of unhealthy love are threatening to those on the receiving end. Most people have at some time experienced the misery of unrequited love, and may even have succumbed to the urge to pester the object of their affections with phone calls and letters or keep an eye on their home or workplace to see what they are up to. However, a small minority of people take this kind of behaviour to abnormal and sometimes dangerous extremes.

In women, the extreme form of unrequited love is known as *erotomania* or *de Clerambault's* syndrome. Apart from its extreme nature, what differentiates this from 'normal' unrequited love is that the sufferer is wrongly convinced that the object of her affections returns her love, and no amount of evidence will shift this delusion. She may, for example, tell herself that he is wearing a tie in her favourite colour as a secret signal that he loves her. The man in question is often someone the woman has encountered in his professional capacity: a doctor, company director or bank manager, who has perhaps helped her in some way and who may be out of her reach socially. Often surfacing in women in their thirties, such a passion frequently leads to bizarre behaviour – phoning, following and writing to the man constantly, harassing his partner and children and, occasionally, even physical attacks. In a few tragic cases, the man's partner has been murdered in the belief that this will remove the last obstacle to their union. It has been suggested that the character played by Glenn Close in the film *Fatal Attraction* was suffering from this kind of abnormal love, although in that instance she had in fact had a sexual relationship with her 'victim' – an important difference.

It is difficult for the man who is pursued by a woman whom he knows either only very slightly or not at all to know how best to respond. If he is able to feel sorry for his tormentor and so show her even the smallest kindness, this will be taken as further evidence that he does love her. If their behaviour becomes threatening such women will be taken to court but, sadly, even this is unlikely to make them see reason, and the condition is very hard to treat successfully.

## Stalkers

A variation on this problem, and one that is more likely to affect women, is the stalker syndrome, although men can be victims too. (Male celebrities are particularly at risk – both Sylvester Stallone and Michael J Fox have been tormented by women stalkers.) While not underestimating the effect on their victims of the strange behaviour of women who pursue men in this way, they are generally less likely than male stalkers to offer a physical threat. Another important difference is that, unlike female stalkers, who create a fantasy affair with their target, male stalkers are often the rejected lovers of the women they pursue.

An analysis by Home Office researchers of figures collected in the British Crime Survey published in October 2000 shows that around 900,000 people suffered the attentions of a stalker during the preceding year.[17] Over half were subjected to violence or had reason to fear that they might be. Women faced double the risk that men faced, and those aged between 16 and 19 were most likely to complain of being stalked. For the majority of victims, being followed, physically intimidated and receiving unwanted, often silent, phone calls were the main problem, but one in four men said they had been assaulted or threatened with violence and one in five women reported physical harassment.

According to the authors of a recent report, stalkers who are former lovers of the women they harass are more likely to use physical violence against their victims. The team analysed the details of 50 stalkers caught or investigated by police in north London during a five-year period. Twenty of the men had had a sexual relationship with their victims and 14 of them had made a violent attack on their former partners. Of the remainder, of whom 18 knew their victims slightly while the rest were complete strangers, only eight had used any form of physical violence. The acquaintances and strangers were more likely to be suffering from a psychotic illness – 22 as compared with only three of the ex-lovers. Interviewed by *The Times*'s medical correspondent, Dr David James, a forensic psychiatrist and one of the report's authors, suggested that 'the vast majority of these people who attack former sexual partners are inadequate people who do not know how to conduct human relations. The likeliest reason for resorting to violence is revenge and an inability to cope with rejection'.[18]

The idea that many male stalkers are men whose own relationships have failed is confirmed by an overview of the topic carried out in 1998 by Karen Abrams and Gail Robinson.[19] Their results suggest that as many as 1 in 20 women may be on the receiving end of a stalker's attentions during their lifetime: attentions that may range from surveillance to threatened or actual violence.

Paul Mullen and his colleagues at Monash University in Victoria, Australia, proposed that stalkers may be classified into one of five categories, although there is some overlap[20]:

- *Rejected stalkers*: almost always focus on a former sexual partner, refusing to accept that the relationship is over and claiming to want reconciliation. This may be combined with a desire for revenge, so the stalker sometimes tries to appease his victim and sometimes is aggressive.

- *Intimacy seekers*: believe themselves in love with an idealised version of someone they have never been close to and often have never met. Despite this, they believe the person does or one day will return their love and refuse to recognise their victim's indifference or distress. They often focus on celebrities or someone they have encountered in that person's professional capacity.
- *Incompetent suitors*: often people lacking in social skills who pursue an uninterested acquaintance in the belief that they have a right to a relationship with that person. If they abandon one target they may repeat their behaviour with a different person.
- *Resentful stalkers*: deliberately create fear and anxiety in their targets in what they see as a justifiable campaign to avenge a perceived injustice or humiliation. Their victims are most likely to be organisations or individuals against whom they harbour some resentment – such as ex-employers or public officials – rather than objects of romantic love or desire.
- *Predatory stalkers*: often spend weeks or months observing a target and planning an attack, which is usually intended to be sexual in nature. They will not normally reveal themselves in advance of the attack but take pleasure in voyeurism and the sense of power and control that stalking gives them.

In some well-publicised cases, the victims have been women in the public eye, pursued by men they have never met who claimed to be in love with them. Olympic skating star Katarina Witt was threatened in letters, top tennis player Monica Seles was stabbed by a man obsessed with Steffi Graf, who felt that Seles threatened her domination of the game, and John Hinckley, who shot President Ronald Reagan, said he did it to impress the actress Jodie Foster. Like Hinckley, the men who act in this way often have few or no relationships in the real world and may be suffering from personality disorders or mental illness.

While stalking and erotomania are far removed from most people's idea of love, the pain of rejection by a lover can sometimes cause people to behave in uncharacteristic ways. Newspaper headlines relating how abandoned women have taken their revenge may even make us smile, as with the woman who gave away the contents of an errant husband's wine cellar to the neighbours and cut up his expensive suits. Yet they serve to remind us that extreme behaviour is not the exclusive preserve of the mad and the bad; being rejected by someone we love can temporarily unbalance even the sanest person, creating the potential for acts of revenge they would not contemplate in more rational times.

# 10

# In the bedroom

*What men desire is a virgin who is also a whore.*

Edward Dahlberg[1]

In the early stages of a relationship, sexual desire is almost always an important and prominent feature and the couple want to make love as often as possible. Sexual arousal and the sexual act itself stimulate the release of hormones and other bodily chemicals that enhance excitement and contribute to the 'high' of being in love. As a general rule, the more sex you have the more you want and the more you experience loving feelings towards your partner. This scenario of frequent, satisfying sex as a vital and happy part of a relationship is constantly reinforced by almost everything we see, hear and read about and even if we are not consciously aware of it, most of us internalise the idea that without good sex a relationship is on the skids.

If sex ceases to be enjoyable or becomes a rare event or, worse still, something either or both partners feel obliged to do, a couple may fear that they are failing one another and that their relationship is doomed. They assume that everyone else is having a great time in bed and are often reluctant to discuss their own situation, either with each other or anyone else. However, this view does not reflect the reality of many relationships; the role of sex within a long-term relationship can change over time and almost certainly will not continue at the same pitch of excitement associated with its beginning.

## Does familiarity breed contempt?

As far back as the 1950s, research demonstrated that repeated exposure to what was termed a positive stimulus resulted in an increasingly diminished emotional response to that stimulus. Most people could cite examples from their own experience: going off a favourite food through eating it too often, becoming sick of a once-loved piece of music through endless repetition and so on. Other researchers have attempted to test whether the same principle applies to sexual stimuli. For example, Kelley and Musialowski found that repeated exposure to an erotic stimulus resulted in the subjects experiencing a decreasing level of reaction towards that stimulus.[2] Introducing a new stimulus revived the subjects so that they viewed it with excitement and a more positive response. A similar effect was seen in a study of long-term relationships, which reported that sexual interest in a partner tended to decline in couples who had been together for a long time.[3]

The mechanism involved may be similar to that which promotes incest avoidance. Research with both animals and humans in a kibbutz situation points up the fact that continuous exposure to the same individual reduces sexual interest. Religious and societal prohibitions may reinforce the incest taboo but we seldom actually need them. Unfortunately, something similar to the incest taboo seems to operate within unrelated couples who spend a great deal of time together. They may continue to love each other but find it difficult to get 'turned on'.

If, as some have suggested, the changes in body chemistry that fuel and sustain early sexual passion do not outlast the first three years or so of a relationship, it is to be expected that this will be reflected in a couple's sex life. Even couples who are still close and loving after several years together rarely exchange passionate embraces every time they meet and part as they probably did at one time. This is not to imply that all passion is spent, but simply to recognise that the couple may no longer feel the need to express their sexual feelings for one another at every opportunity. Sex has not exactly taken a back seat but it has come to occupy a different and less prominent place within their relationship. In terms of chemistry, the bonding chemicals oxytocin and vasopressin have taken over the leading roles from those that triggered excitement and desire, so encouraging the transition from the dizzy euphoria of being 'in love' to less dramatic but more deeply rooted feelings of love for the partner. This could be said to be the ideal situation and is, in fact, what actually happens with many couples who do succeed in maintaining a happy and close relationship over a period of years.

Things do not work out that way for everyone, however. Once the initial excitement has faded, it may be replaced by boredom or feelings of disappointment with one another, which will usually be reflected in sexual difficulties or conflict. Although, as we mentioned earlier, there is considerable evidence suggesting that humans easily become bored in the absence of new sources of excitement and stimulation, in real life some couples deal with this more effectively than others. In the 1960s, a US research project showed that couples who were able to enjoy a range of activities together were more likely to stay happily married than those who didn't.[4] This conclusion is probably just as relevant today as it was then, although, of course, spending time apart and pursuing separate interests may be as much a symptom of marital difficulty as a cause.

## Misunderstandings

The idea that male desire is more urgent and uncomplicated than female desire has been around for many years. Nature, it is argued, has arranged things so that men respond primarily to visual stimuli and are easily sexually aroused, whereas for women sex is more closely linked to the emotions. This implies that men are much more able to gain sexual satisfaction with any desirable partner: love need have nothing to do with it. Women, on the other hand, tend to compound the two and rarely respond to visual stimuli alone. This is why, it is said, no one has managed to successfully market soft porn magazines for women in imitation of the many such publications aimed at men. In terms of evolutionary biology, this way of differentiating between male and female perspectives on sex does make sense and is no doubt true as a generalisation. Women and men also tend to express their disappointment with unsatisfying sex lives in different terms. Whereas women are more likely to complain that their partners are insufficiently warm, loving and caring, men are more concerned about what they see as a lack of variety and about not having sex often enough.[5] However, as we saw in Chapter 8, recent work by sociobiologists has suggested that women also have much to gain, in terms of getting the best possible genetic inheritance for their children, by having more than one sexual partner. The female orgasm may not, it seems, be biologically redundant (as was long believed) and it is therefore in women's reproductive interests as much as it is in men's to pursue sexual pleasure. Love need have nothing to do with it for them either, according to this argument.

It is not necessary to reject this analysis of inbuilt biologically driven sexual characteristics to argue that there is more to human sexual relations than satisfying the 'demands' of our genes to be passed on to the next generation. Whatever complex links may exist between genes, emotions and personality, people do not regard themselves as robots programmed to behave in certain fixed ways and bring other factors to bear in their dealings with other people and, especially, with lovers. There is increasing evidence that men are beginning to make the same protests against being treated purely as sex objects as women have been doing for decades. One recent sign of changing times was an interview given to a tabloid newspaper in September 2000 by the estranged husband of Spice Girl Mel B. According to Jimmy Gulzar, he lost interest in having sex with his wife because of other differences between them, which left him with the sense that his feelings did not count with her. As he apparently put it, 'If my head ain't right, my willy ain't right'.[6] Just the previous week, the same newspaper featured a similar story from a man who complained that his ex-girlfriend only wanted him for his body. According to a letter written by this man, 'I need to be appreciated, and not just because I can give you an orgasm'.[7]

Of course, such stories cannot be taken as evidence of changing views among men in general, but studies carried out on behalf of the relationship counselling service Relate offer some confirmation that the trend may be genuine. Increasing numbers of men are seeking help from the organisation because they have lost interest in having sex with their partners – not because they were physically unable to do so but for personal reasons, including a sense that something had gone awry within the relationship as a whole. According to the Relate findings, the percentage of men consulting the organisation because of this kind of difficulty has risen from 7–8 per cent in 1996 to around 15 per cent in the most recent analysis. Commenting to *The Guardian*, Julia Cole, a Relate-trained couples counsellor, said: 'My experience in therapy over 12 years is that when you talk to men, they may start by saying they want more sex. But what they say after a while is that they want to be touched and caressed in the same way as their partners'.[8]

## Sex as a barometer

Sometimes a couple may feel that the only thing that is good about their relationship is their sex life. Even when they are fighting about all manner of other things or seem to have little else in common, they may continue to get on surprisingly well in the bedroom. However, such people are probably in a minority and sexual difficulties or dissatisfaction are often the result of problems elsewhere in the relationship. As Sarah Litvinoff puts it: 'Good sex is not a cure for all relationship problems, although if you are giving each other sexual pleasure it will help you to feel good about each other. Unsatisfying sex might have a purely physical cause, but it is just as likely to be a symptom of other things that are not satisfying in your relationship'.[9]

Evidence to support this view comes from a study that involved both happily married couples and couples who were receiving counselling.[10] The happy couples had sex more frequently than the ones with problems, but they also reported enjoying many other activities together. As Eliot Smith and Diane Mackie have pointed out, results of this kind are hard to interpret. It may be that 'sexual activity increases relationship satisfaction, but it could also mean that couples who are generally satisfied with their relationship have intercourse more often'.[11] Consistent with this is the fact that certain personality traits in one's partner (being disagreeable, emotionally unstable and closed-minded) are known to make for marital and sexual dissatisfaction.[12] Women with borderline personality disorder are also more likely to be depressed and dissatisfied with their sex lives.[13] Apparently, relationships depend partly on personality compatibility and when the relationship suffers, so does the couple's sexual satisfaction.

According to Litvinoff, identifying what might be wrong in a couple's relationship involves consideration of all aspects of their lives together and the way they relate to each other. These can range from division of labour within the home, money management and joint activities and interests to how much each partner likes and respects the other and the way they handle disagreements. She points out that failure to tackle issues that seem important to one or both partners can generate angry feelings, which may or may not be openly expressed but which nevertheless can have repercussions on a couple's sex life.

Relationship counsellors who spend time with troubled couples often find that what may sound like relatively trivial complaints mask more deep-seated and fundamental problems. For example, a woman who complains that her partner has gained weight and become careless about his appearance may really be feeling resentful because he spends so much time drinking with his friends and gives her little of his time or attention. Similarly, a man who complains that his partner is more interested in her career than in him may actually be feeling undermined because she is earning more than him or because, unlike him, she has a job she enjoys. Disagreements of this kind may be affecting more and more relationships as a result of changing social conditions in Western countries. Women in particular expect more from a relationship than did their mothers and grandmothers and, in many cases, have more freedom to exercise lifestyle choices. If, as some argue, human evolution has equipped men to be the providers and women to be the home-makers and child-carers, there is likely to be conflict when individuals choose to break this pattern and make different arrangements for themselves. It would be surprising if such conflict were not reflected in couples' sexual responses to one another since these, too, have evolved over millions of years.

An interesting approach to assessing the importance of sex as a factor in marital satisfaction was adopted in a study at the University of Oregon by John Howard and Robyn Dawes.[14] They discovered that while the rate of sexual intercourse in married couples or the frequency of their arguments do not by themselves relate very much to marital happiness, the difference between them does so very well. Nearly all couples who describe their marriages as 'happy' have intercourse more often than they have arguments, whereas nearly all couples who regard their marriage as 'unhappy' argue more often than they have intercourse. Therefore, Howard and Dawes propose the following simple formula:

Marital happiness = rate of intercourse – rate of argument

Intercourse was defined as 'genital union with or without orgasm', while an argument was defined as any occasion on which at least one party became uncooperative, including physical attack or departure, verbal attack or withdrawal or emotional outbursts. Howard and Dawes found that couples with consistently negative scores based on this formula are likely to separate or divorce within a reasonably short space of time.

## Beware the curse

One factor that often causes conflict within a partnership is the man's adverse reaction to the premenstrual phase of the woman's cycle. Because irritability arising out of hormonal conditions is not always recognised as such, it can put a considerable strain on the relationship. An interesting way of countering this detrimental effect is called *conjoint monitoring*. Beth Frank *et al* found that when husband and wife charted cyclic symptoms together there was an improvement in sexual satisfaction, general communication and contentment.[15] Presumably this came about because the menstrual symptoms could more readily be seen for what they actually were, with a resulting reduction in attributions to the behaviour of the husband (leading inevitably to rows).

It is interesting to speculate that disruption of relationships could be the evolutionary intent of premenstrual syndrome. Just as morning sickness in pregnancy has recently been recognised as a mechanism for protecting the foetus from food toxins like coffee, so it is reasonable to ask what might be the survival value of premenstrual irritability; simple hormonal disturbance is not a functional explanation. One possibility is that, finding herself not pregnant (which would be the normal state of a fertile woman in ancestral times), she reacts by 'rocking the boat' so as to increase the likelihood of moving on to a different (potentially more fertile) male in time for her next ovulation. Such irascible behaviour could thus serve gene survival. At the very least, it would severely test the present partner's loyalty and devotion. As with all evolutionary tricks, there is no reason to expect that the woman herself would have any conscious appreciation of why her body is behaving in this way.

## Parents and sex

Although the link between sex and parenthood is direct and obvious, modern Western societies tend to create an artificial separation between the two, with the emphasis very much on sex. Women's bodies, and their breasts in particular, are portrayed in the media in a highly sexualised way, with little or no reference to their reproductive and child-nurturing functions. We may no longer see half-naked women draped across car bonnets in ads designed to sell to men, but few people bat an eyelid at gargantuan images of women's breasts – such as in the famous 'Hello boys' series of bra advertisements that appeared on bus shelters and roadside posters all over the UK recently. Apart from the specialist press, most popular media coverage of pregnancy, birth and motherhood confines itself to 'rosy-glow' pictures of new mums (and sometimes dads) cuddling smiling, sleepy babies, or comments intrusively on the way celebrities such as Madonna or Posh Spice have (or have not) regained their figures after having a baby. As far as their public image is concerned, breasts are discussed in terms of their size and shape (enhanced or reduced), whether or not they are currently fashionable and portrayed exclusively as part of a woman's sexual armoury; one thing they are not is providers of food for a baby.

There is little open discussion of whether and how becoming parents affects a couple's sex life; rather it is assumed by most people before they experience it for themselves that everything will just go back to the way it was before within a relatively short period after the birth. A moment's thought will suggest many reasons why this is unlikely to be the reality for most new parents, yet many are troubled and disappointed when they discover that the arrival of a baby has an enormous and unwelcome effect on their sexual relationship.

A recent survey conducted among readers of *Practical Parenting* magazine pointed up many of the common problems.[16] Three-quarters of women who replied to the questionnaire said that they had lost interest in sex for a time after the birth of their babies. The reasons included sheer exhaustion, which was a big factor particularly for mothers aged between 24 and 33. Younger mothers were more inclined to cite physical discomfort as a reason for avoiding sex. Around three-quarters had had sex again by three months after the birth, although, interestingly, some admitted that they had done so without actually wanting to (presumably to please their partners). There were also some interesting reactions reported on the part of new fathers. While 77 per cent were understanding the first time their partners turned them down when they wanted sex, they became more grudging if the refusals were repeated. Fewer than half continued to accept the situation with a good grace, around a third did so grudgingly and 14 per cent sulked. Although the majority of respondents did resume their sex lives within a few months of having a baby, over half reported that it was not as good as before, with only 17 per cent reporting an actual improvement. Tiredness and lack of time to spend together as a couple were put forward as reasons by many, but 1 in 10 put the change down to one partner seeming to be less interested in having sex with the other – split evenly between men and women as the one said to have lost interest.

While it is true that for many new parents, tiredness and lack of time to spend together are the main obstacles in the way of resuming their sexual relationship, other less obvious factors may be playing their part too. Hormonal changes following the birth may well affect a woman's sexual responsiveness, especially if she is breast-feeding. As we saw in Chapter 4, oxytocin helps to stimulate sexual desire and encourages feelings of closeness to a partner, but it is also responsible for triggering the milk 'let down' response in a woman who is breast-feeding. Some women find feeding their baby sexually arousing, but many others find any sexual touching of their breasts uncomfortable or off-putting at this time. Stimulating the breasts may cause milk to start flowing, which some women and men find disturbing – perhaps because it is 'messy' or because it points up the potential conflict between the role of mother and that of lover. As Juliet Rix puts it: 'Culturally, motherhood is at the opposite end of the spectrum from the "loose woman"; the ideal of motherhood being represented by the virgin mother of Christ.'[17] She suggests that many women have subconsciously absorbed the idea that there is something wrong with mothers being sexual and that this, combined with the day-to-day reality of caring for a child, can sometimes make it difficult to switch from one role to the other. Rix points out that some people may need to make a special effort to 'retain an image of each other as individual adults as well as parents. Calling each other "Mummy" and "Daddy" to the children makes obvious sense, but some couples fall into the trap of continuing this in private, often adding to the parent/partner confusion'.

Whether a diminished or non-existent sex life following the birth of a child is a serious problem depends on individual couples. Relationship counsellors stress that it need not become important if the couple are still able to communicate and find other, non-sexual ways of fostering their intimacy. If parents are content to allow themselves time to adjust to their new role and believe that sex will naturally become a part of their lives when both are ready, there is no need for concern. However, if the relationship as a whole is being adversely affected by the lack of sex or if one partner starts to feel frustrated enough to consider having sex with someone else, the problem does need to be tackled.

If the individuals concerned find it difficult to know how to begin putting things right between them, they may benefit from advice from a trained therapist or counsellor, such as those operating under the auspices of Relate. If appropriate, a *sensate focus* programme may be suggested, a method originally developed by William Masters and Virginia Johnson, the American pioneers of the study of sexuality. Although it concentrates on physical contact and sensation, the programme requires high levels of intimacy and communication between the two people concerned, and thus often brings underlying, not specifically sexual, differences and problems into the open. The programme is divided into two separate stages, each of which can last for an unlimited period of time. The first involves non-sexual touching and gives each partner a chance to discover what kind of touch they enjoy as well as what pleases their partner. In the second phase, genital touching, the couple again take turns to be giver and receiver, although they are usually advised not to have full penetrative sex. For many couples, participating in the programme, especially under the guidance of a sex therapist, is the key to discovering (or re-discovering) a satisfying sex life, but it can also sometimes reveal unbridgeable gaps or deep-seated problems within a relationship.

## Drugs and aphrodisiacs

The idea that a flagging sex life can be instantly revived if one or both partners take some miraculous pill or potion has been around for centuries. Despite the reputation of a whole range of substances – from ground rhino horn to Spanish fly, from oysters to synthetic pheromones – their supposed efficacy is largely an illusion. Most of them have no useful effect whatever and some may even be toxic, including Spanish fly and amyl nitrate (poppers). Even if any of them did actually have practical benefits, such as improving an erection or encouraging lubrication, there is more to achieving a satisfying sex life than the ability to perform.

Viagra (oral sildenafil) may be an exception to this rule. This relatively new drug can help certain categories of men to achieve and sustain an erection when they would not be able to do so without it. In the UK, it can be prescribed on the National Health Service only for men whose impotence has certain physiological causes, such as blood vessel or nerve damage resulting from diabetes or spinal cord injury. However, it can be obtained on a private prescription in some instances and is widely advertised for sale on the Internet, where it is promoted as a way for men who are not impotent to prolong their erections. However, using such a powerful drug without medical advice is potentially dangerous.

For those men for whom it is the right treatment, it can help to make intercourse possible, but it will not help all men with erectile difficulties nor will it solve sexual problems that have their underlying cause in the relationship itself. As we have seen, problems in the bedroom are often the result of unresolved difficulties between the couple concerned – they are a symptom rather than a cause of trouble between them. In a study carried out in an outpatients clinic, 58 men aged between 21 and 75 suffering from erection difficulties were treated with Viagra.[18] It was a complete success for 43 per cent, who were able to have intercourse afterwards, but the rest continued to have some problems, including 17 per cent who did not benefit at all. The authors of the study conclude that, while it provides more evidence of the drug's effectiveness, it also shows that some men will need other types of treatment in addition.

There have been suggestions that Viagra might also be given to women with sexual difficulties caused by lack of physical arousal, although it is generally agreed that such problems often have emotional and psychological elements that would be unaffected by a purely physical therapy. However, a group of nine women with problems achieving orgasm following treatment with SSRI (Prozac-type) anti-depressants experienced significant improvements after taking Viagra, mostly after just one dose.[19]

Alcohol has long held a reputation as an aphrodisiac although, as the porter in Shakespeare's *Macbeth* explains so pithily, it is unreliable in this respect:

'Lechery it provokes and unprovokes.
It provokes the desire but takes away the performance.'

In fact, alcohol is more of a central depressant than a stimulant. The main effect of drinking alcohol is to release inhibitions but its effects on the nervous system also result in diminished sensation. One study that looked at alcohol in relation to sexual behaviour suggested that one of the main reasons why people are more willing to have sex when they've been drinking is that they can then blame it for the fact that they behaved in ways that they would not have done if sober.[20]

Regular users of marijuana claim that it is effective in

enhancing sexual pleasure and as an aphrodisiac. Of 60 male and 37 female subjects studied by Ronald Weller and James Halikas, over two-thirds said their sexual satisfaction and pleasure were increased by their use of the drug and half said it increased their desire for their regular partner.[21] In particular, they felt that sensations of touch and taste were powerfully increased. The majority of those interviewed had used marijuana before having sex, one in five doing so regularly. However, the long-term side effects of marijuana are little known and a matter of some concern.

## Hormone replacement therapy

As a woman approaches the menopause, levels of the female hormones oestrogen and progesterone decline and eventually production stops altogether. For many women, this causes few or no problems but for some there may be both physical and psychological effects, which can interfere with their desire for and enjoyment of sex. In particular, low levels of oestrogen can result in vaginal dryness, which makes sexual intercourse uncomfortable or even painful. Mood changes and depression trouble some women at this time, although this may be due to their feelings about themselves rather than a direct physical consequence of hormonal changes. If sex has always been associated with the possibility, however theoretical, of conception the knowledge that this is no longer the case may cause a woman to lose interest in it. For some women, the menopause is a sign that they are no longer sexual beings or even desirable, although for others it may be a kind of liberation to know that they can enjoy sex with no possibility of pregnancy. Hormone replacement therapy (HRT), which involves taking synthetic female hormones, can alleviate many physical symptoms and may help to lift mood but it is not right for everyone and the pros and cons must be weighed on an individual basis by each woman and her doctor.

Despite publicity about the concept of the 'male menopause', men do not experience the same kind of hormonal changes as women although they can and do experience similar emotions related to feelings about getting older and changes in their self-image. Although levels of the male hormone testosterone do decline with age, only the small minority of men whose levels fall sufficiently will benefit from taking a synthetic substitute. Harvey Sternbach acknowledges that symptoms of testosterone deficiency may include depression, lowered sex drive and impotence, but points out that other factors, such as physical diseases like diabetes, and psychological stresses may also be involved.[22] He argues that men with low testosterone levels should be carefully assessed before hormone replacement is considered and that more research is needed into its long-term safety and efficacy. The same cautions should be applied to the potential benefits for some post-menopausal women of treatment with testosterone in conjunction with ordinary HRT. One study reported that three women who had low testosterone levels following surgical removal of their uterus and ovaries regained their sexual energy following treatment with low doses of synthetic testosterone.[23]

While replacing oestrogen and progesterone can help to improve the sex lives of some women during and after the menopause, HRT is not a panacea. This is even more true of testosterone, which may be an appropriate therapy for a minority of individuals but is clearly not the answer to diminishing libido or ability to have sexual intercourse as far as the majority of people are concerned. The solutions must be looked for elsewhere, perhaps in personal, psychosexual or relationship counselling.

# 11

# Hope over experience

*Marriage is the tomb of love.*

Casanova

According to Oscar Wilde, a second marriage represents 'the triumph of hope over experience'. Yet people do embark on second – or even subsequent – marriages or move from one long-term relationship into another, confident that this time, it will be different. Statistics suggest that, in the majority of cases, this confidence is misplaced. Whereas about half of all first marriages in the United States end in divorce, the comparable figure for second marriages is 80 per cent.[1] In Britain, both figures are lower but proportionately similar. Obviously, these startling statistics don't include the number of long-term relationships that break up without the couples concerned ever having married.

## Risk factors

Various risk factors have been put forward to explain why subsequent marriages are even more likely to break down than first marriages. These include pressures created by society, unequal exchanges (such as older men marrying much younger women, or vice versa) and personality traits that predict the tendency to divorce, whether in a first or subsequent marriage.

In Chapter 5, we looked at attachment theory, which proposes that people can be categorised as adopting one of three attachment styles (although there may be some overlap): secure, anxious and avoidant. One study aimed to relate attachment style to a propensity for multiple marriages.[2] The researchers asked 154 remarried women with an average age of 39 to complete the Adult Attachment Scale to assess their attachment style. The results indicated that those who had been married more than once were more likely to have an avoidant attachment style and less likely to have an anxious attachment style. If an avoidant attachment style contributed to the break-up of the first marriage, then it is likely that, if they continued to adopt the same emotional attitudes and responses in their new partnerships as they had done in previous marriages, the women faced an increased risk of another divorce.

However, it should not be assumed that because second marriages break down more often than first marriages that they are necessarily less happy. The difference may be primarily one of the power of the constraints against divorce.[3] Previously divorced people are better able to contemplate this option if things go wrong; they are also less likely to have children from the second marriage, and it is well known that children can hold together unhappy marriages.

## A clean break?

Few people manage to separate from a long-term partner without some degree of stress and emotional trauma and adjusting to such a significant life change can be a long, difficult and not always successful process. For the separation to become final and complete, various interlinked elements must be disentangled and how successfully this is accomplished will affect subsequent attitudes and relationships. One study identified three separate components that must be dealt with when any relationship breaks up: love for the partner, attachment to established routines and attachment to marital role.[4] According to the authors of the study, how well each of these processes is dealt with by each partner determines whether the divorce is what they term 'orderly' or 'disorderly'. By combining the various ways in which the three types of 'disengagement' are managed by the two individuals, the authors identified different types of disorderly divorce. These range from those where the partners continue much as before ('divorced in name only') to those where one partner still loves the other and still thinks of him- or herself as a spouse ('I wish it hadn't happened'). Failure to successfully disentangle from a former partner – whether on a practical or emotional level or both – is likely to make it more difficult for the individual to move on and to build a successful relationship with a new partner.

In the light of these findings, it is interesting to note the results of a study that looked at the attitudes of older women who had been widowed towards remarriage.[5] The researchers asked 64 widows aged between 61 and 85 how they felt about the idea of marrying again. Although most said they were interested in or attracted to men, the great majority of them said they were opposed to the possibility of a second marriage or thought it would be impossible for them. The author suggested a number of considerations that might account for such views, including the duration and number of previous marriage(s), whether the women were still grieving, whether they worked, finances, age and health. It is perhaps not surprising that women whose marriages ended with the death of a partner relatively late in life might adopt different attitudes towards the prospect of remarriage from women whose marriages had ended in divorce.

## The ex-factor

When a divorced person remarries, they inevitably take a certain amount of emotional 'baggage' with them from the old to the new relationship, some of which will relate to the former spouse. There is evidence that the way couples relate to one another after divorce and the amount of continuing contact between them actually do affect the level of happiness experienced with the new spouse. Elizabeth Stark identified four categories of post-divorce relationships, which she called 'fiery foes', 'angry associates', 'co-operative colleagues' and 'perfect pals'.[6] She suggests that those who are able to stay in regular touch with their former partners tend to have happier second marriages than those who cannot. In particular this may help to facilitate continuing financial support and allow children to remain in touch with both parents. Whether this proves possible in practice can be predicted, says Stark, on the basis of factors such as the nature of a couple's former relationship, the circumstances in which it ended and their attitude to the divorce.

The way in which feelings about former spouses could influence the likely success of the new partnership was examined by Bram Buunk and Wim Mutsaers.[7] Working with 290 remarried people, the researchers found that few continued to be attached to or friends with their former spouse and, although not that widespread, feelings of hostility were a more common experience than friendliness. Individuals who were not parents and those with more education tended to have better relations with their ex-partner. Wives were particularly likely to be dissatisfied with their marriage if their second husband was still attached to his ex-wife. Their own relationship with their ex-spouse was dependent on their husband's approval and the more problems the latter had concerning this relationship, the less satisfied they were with their current marriage.

The lingering death of an earlier marriage appears to threaten the survival of the second, at least in its early years, according to the findings of a study of 749 women who had been divorced and remarried at least once.[8] The subjects had married for the second time between 1965 and 1988; 29 per cent of them expected this relationship to end within five years. However, of those who had had a failed reconciliation with an earlier partner before divorcing, 33 per cent expected their new marriage to fail, compared with 27 per cent of those who had not attempted reconciliation. By the time the women had been in their second or subsequent marriage for 10 years, the gap between the expectations of marriage failure for the two groups had narrowed to 50 per cent and 47 per cent respectively. The author suggests that sociodemographic variables may exert more influence on the likelihood of marriage breakdown during the early phase of the partnership. The results also suggest that a history of attempting reconciliation in the first marriage augurs badly for the survival chances of the second.

In weighing their level of satisfaction in a second or subsequent marriage, people will inevitably use comparisons with their earlier experience as one of their measures. In some respects, it seems that the perceived degree of difference between the present and the past may be particularly significant. In a group of 290 remarried people who were more satisfied with their current marriage than they had been in their previous one, both men and women but especially women perceived a greater degree of equality in the later relationship.[9] The more equitable the relationship, the greater the level of satisfaction. However, the way the balance was seen to have shifted by the men and the women in the study was not exactly the same. The men, on average, claimed to have felt deprived in their first marriage and 'over-benefited' in the second; the greater their sense of being in a position of advantage, the happier they were. The women, on the other hand, were more likely to see their current marriage as more or less equal; the more strongly they felt this, the greater their satisfaction.

Most women – and maybe even some men – will be unsurprised to learn that women spend less time on household chores in a second marriage or live-in relationship than do women in a partnership where both individuals are married or cohabiting for the first time. This conclusion is based on analyses of results from the British Household Panel Study (1991), and applies to women in second marriages and relationships regardless of the number of previous relationships the men concerned may have had.[10] The author concludes that women use the experience and insights drawn from the breakdown of their earlier marriages or relationships to negotiate new arrangements with their next partner. Other research findings have bolstered the theory that some women at least are able to apply lessons learned from a failed marriage to enhance their chances of achieving happiness with their second husband. For example, Lydia Prado and Howard Markham suggest that women learn to manage problems in a relationship more successfully the second time around. According to these authors, it is not the number of problems in a relationship that is significant in leading to relationship breakdown, but the way in which couples are able to communicate to solve them.[11]

## Parents and partners

If, as Shakespeare put it in *A Midsummer Night's Dream*, 'The course of true love never did run smooth', it is even less likely to do so where one or both of the potential lovers must consider the needs and concerns of their children with respect to a new relationship. In earlier generations, a woman with one or more children to care for without a partner would be considered fortunate if she found a man prepared to take her on but, even though attitudes have changed, children may still prove to be a complication when it comes to remarriage.

In the late 1970s, there was an increasing trend for mothers under the age of 30 to marry again within a relatively short time after their divorce.[12] This was particularly true for less educated women. More recent studies in Britain, however, have suggested that the more children a divorced woman has, the less likely it is that she will find a new husband or partner.[13] This finding is based on analyses of data from the General Household Survey, together with interviews with divorced people about their attitudes to remarriage. The authors of the study point out that children may affect the chances of their parent taking on a new partner in a number of ways: by the demands they make on their parent's time and emotions, by objecting to a potential partner or by putting off the individual concerned. From the parent's perspective, caring for their children may be a higher priority than making a new relationship for themselves. The study found that divorced mothers who did want a new relationship were not looking for a father for their children but rather were seeking a partner for themselves. Among formerly married people without children, Lampard and Peggs found that the desire for children was a major motive for seeking a new partner.

Parents and prospective new partners may well be concerned that the experience of their parents' divorce will have adversely affected the children emotionally and psychologically in ways that could make adapting to a step-parent particularly problematic. In fact, there is evidence that behavioural problems in children of divorced parents often appear before the separation actually takes place and are the result of conflict within the relationship rather than of its demise.[14] With respect to remarriage, there is evidence that this is better for the adjustment of a divorced woman's children than just living with a new partner. However, remarriage was not superior to remaining single as far as children's adjustment is concerned.[15]

## The way ahead

With the ongoing rise in the numbers of people living without a partner, it may be that the single lifestyle will increasingly come to be seen as a desirable option, deliberately chosen in preference to marriage or live-in relationships by many adults. Choosing to live alone does not, of course, necessarily preclude having a lover or sexual relationship, nor does it rule out parenthood. For some the advantages of living alone may appear to outweigh any disadvantages.

Back in 1982, Leonard Cargan and Matthew Melko studied a group of people in Dayton, Ohio of whom 29 per cent had never been married, 9 per cent were divorced, 55 per cent had been married once and 11 per cent were remarried (the figures were rounded up where appropriate). They also analysed 603 questionnaires completed by members of a singles organisation. Cargan and Melko reported that while singles expressed less overall happiness than marrieds, they apparently also had more fun – as defined by experiences such as outings or sexual variety. Single people were more likely to be lonely or depressed but married people reported more symptoms of stress such as headaches, insomnia, ulcers and high blood pressure. However, the majority of singles (whether or not they had been married before) expected that they would be marrying within the next five years.[16]

A more recent study looked at single women aged between 30 and 65 to assess their attitudes to their single state.[17] This also revealed ambivalent attitudes about the reasons why they were single. Most perceived that their situation offered both advantages as well as drawbacks. Although expressing themselves content to remain single, they also experienced feelings of loss and grief with respect to this aspect of their lives.

However, there is growing evidence that the lack of a committed relationship with a man does not rule out successful motherhood, at least for those women in higher income and educational brackets who are likely to have fewer hurdles to jump in terms of finance and paid childcare. The traditional stereotype of the single mother presented her as coping only with great difficulty and in the face of social disapproval, but a recent study paints a different picture.[18] The women interviewed, all of whom were financially independent and well educated, reported that their decision to become single mothers had been made with the support of family, friends, physicians and employers, who accepted this non-traditional family structure as a viable choice.

While such tolerance of unconventional life choices is certainly not universal, it does reflect an increasing acceptance that a committed and exclusive partnership with a person of the opposite sex is no longer the *sine qua non* of social acceptability. Some individuals will always prefer marriage or a committed one-to-one partnership, while others may opt for serial relationships, gay partnerships, single living, shared households with others who are friends rather than sexual partners, or even a 'swinging' lifestyle where sexual relationships are openly accepted outside the prime pairing. Such unconventional arrangements have always existed, of course, albeit often concealed from the rest of society, just as people have always continued to fall in and out of love.

It is hard to imagine that, in Western societies at least, lifelong marriage will ever reclaim its lost status as the only acceptable lifestyle choice but it is equally impossible to imagine that human beings will ever learn to resist the joys and desolation of love, wherever it may lead them.

# References

Chapter 1
Illusion and reality

[1] Anderson, S (1986) *Death in the Woods*, W W Norton & Company, USA

[2] Rubin, Z (1988) Introduction, in *The Psychology of Love*, ed R J Sternberg and M L Barnes, Yale University Press, New Haven, CT

[3] Rubin, Z (1970) 'Measurement of romantic love', *Journal of Personality and Social Psychology*, **16**, pp 265–73

[4] Knox, D, Zusman, M and Nieves, W (1998) 'What I did for love: risky behavior of college students in love', *College Student Journal*, **32**, pp 203–05

[5] Aron, E N and Aron, A (1997) 'Extremities of love: the sudden sacrifice of career, family, dignity', *Journal of Social and Clinical Psychology*, **16**, pp 200–12

[6] Lamm, H and Weissmann, U (1997) 'Subjective attributes of attraction: how people characterise their love, and their being in love', *Personal Relationships*, **4**, pp 271–84

[7] Hatfield, E and Walster, G W (1978) *A New Look at Love*, Addison-Wesley, Reading, MA

[8] Tennov, D (1973) *Love and Limerence*, Stein and Day, New York, NY

[9] Brenner, M (1971) 'Caring, love and selective memory', *Proceedings of the Annual Convention of the American Psychological Association*, **6**, pp 275–76

[10] Brandon, N (1988) A vision of romantic love, in *The Psychology of Love*, ed R J Sternberg and M L Barnes, Yale University Press, New Haven, CT

[11] Lee, J A (1976) *Lovestyles*, J M Dent, London

[12] Hatkoff, T and Lasswell, T E (1979) Male-female differences and similarities in conceptualising love, in *Love and Attraction: An International Conference*, ed M Cook and G D Wilson, Pergamon, Oxford

[13] Wilson, G D and Nias, D K B (1976) *Love's Mysteries: The Psychology of Sexual Attraction*, Open Books, London

[14] Kephart, W M (1967) 'Some correlates of romantic love', *Journal of*

*Marriage and the Family*, **29**, pp 470–78

[15] Montgomery, M J and Sorell, G T (1998) 'Love and dating experience in early and middle adolescence: grade and gender comparisons', *Journal of Adolescence*, **21**, pp 677–89

[16] Byrne, D (1999) *Exploring Social Psychology*, 4th edn, Allyn and Bacon, Boston, MA

[17] Lee, J A (1998) Ideologies of lovestyle and sexstyle, in *Romantic Love and Sexual Behavior*, ed V C De Munck *et al*, Praeger Publishers/Greenwood Publishing Group, Westport, CT

[18] Yelsma, P and Athappilly, K (1988) 'Marital satisfaction and communication practices: comparisons among Indian and American couples', *Journal of Comparative Family Studies*, **19**, pp 37–54

[19] Derne, S (1977) Structural realities, persistent dilemmas, and the construction of emotional paradigms, in *Social Perspectives on Emotion*, Vol 2, ed W M Wentworth *et al*, Jai Press Inc., Greenwich, CT

## Chapter 2
## Beauty and sex appeal

[1] *Getting Even* (1973)

[2] Etcoff, N (1999) *Survival of the Prettiest*, Little and Brown, New York, NY

[3] Zebrowitz, L A (1997) *Reading Faces: Window to the Soul?*, Westview Press, Oxford

[4] Perrett, D I (1998) 'Effects of sexual dimorphism on facial attractiveness', *Nature*, **394**, pp 884–87

[5] Dunbar, R *et al* (2000) 'Nature', cited in *The Times*, 13 January 2000

[6] Wildt, L and Sir-Peterman, T (1999) 'Oestrogen and age estimations of perimenopausal women', *The Lancet*, **354**, p 224

[7] Singh, D (1993) 'Adaptive significance of female physical attractiveness: role of waist-to-hip ratio', *Journal of Personality and Social Psychology*, **65**, pp 293–307

[8] Henss, R (2000) 'Waist-to-hip ratio and female attractiveness: evidence from photographic stimuli and methodological considerations', *Personality and Individual Differences*, **28**, pp 501–03

[9] Wilson, G D and Nias, D K B (1976) *Love's Mysteries: The Psychology of Sexual Attraction*, Open Books, London

[10] Feinman, S and Gill, G W (1978) 'Sex differences in physical

References

attractiveness and preferences', *Journal of Social Psychology*, **100**, pp 46–52

[11] Weir, S and Fine, D M (1989) 'Dumb blonde and temperamental redhead', *Irish Journal of Psychology*, **10**, pp 11–19

[12] Clayson, D E and Maughan, M R (1984) 'Redheads and blonds: stereotypic images', *Psychological Reports*, **59**, pp 811–16

[13] Lalumière, M L (1999) Proceedings of the Royal Society, cited in *The Times*, 9 December 1999

[14] Thornhill, R, Gangestad, S W and Comer, R (1995) 'Human female orgasm and mate fluctuating asymmetry', *Animal Behaviour*, **50**, pp 1601–15

[15] See Reference 2

[16] Dutton, D G and Aron, A P (1974) 'Some evidence for heightened sexual attraction under conditions of high anxiety', *Journal of Personality and Social Psychology*, **30**, pp 510–17

[17] Valins, S (1971) 'Cognitive effects of false heart rate feedback', *Journal of Personality of Social Psychology*, **4**, pp 400–08

[18] White, G L *et al* (1981) 'Passionate love and the misattribution of arousal', *Journal of Personality and Social Psychology*, **41**, pp 56–62

[19] Foster, C A *et al* (1998) 'Arousal and attraction: evidence for automatic and controlled processes', *Journal of Personality and Social Psychology*, **74**, pp 86–101

[20] *The Star*, 18 January 1988

[21] Turnbull, J (1999) 'Forbidden desires', *The Times*, 5 January 1999

[22] Kendrick, K M *et al* (1998) 'Mothers determine sexual preference', *Nature*, **395**, pp 229–30

[23] Wilson, G D and Barrett, P N (1987) 'Parental characteristics and partner choice: some evidence for Oedipal imprinting', *Journal of Biosocial Science*, **19**, pp 157–61

[24] Bateson, P (1978) 'Sexual imprinting and optimal outbreeding', *Nature*, **273**, pp 259–60

Chapter 3
Take your partners

[1] Hess, E H (1965) 'Attitude and pupil size', *Scientific American*, **212**, pp 46–54

[2] Aronson, E and Linder, D (1965) 'Gain and loss of esteem as determinants of interpersonal attractiveness', *Journal of Experimental Social*

*Psychology*, **1**, pp 156–71

[3] Walster, E *et al* (1973) '"Playing hard to get": understanding an elusive phenomenon', *Journal of Personality and Social Psychology*, **26**, pp 113–21

[4] Clark, R D and Hatfield, E (1989) 'Gender differences in receptivity to sexual offers', *Journal of Psychology and Human Sexuality*, **2**, pp 39–55

[5] Buss, D M (1999) *Evolutionary Psychology: The New Science of the Mind*, Allyn & Bacon, Needham Heights, MA

[6] Lalumière, M L, Seto, M C and Quinsey, V L (1995) Self-perceived mating success and the mating choices of human males and females, in *Evolutionary Psychology: The New Science of the Mind*, ed D M Buss, Allyn & Bacon, Needham Heights, MA

[7] Baize, H R and Schroeder, J E (1995) 'Personality and mate selection in personal ads: evolutionary preferences in public mate selection process', *Journal of Social Behavior and Personality*, **10**, pp 517–36

[8] Lance, L M (1998) 'Gender differences in heterosexual dating: a content analysis of personal ads', *Journal of Men's Studies*, **6** (3), pp 297–305

[9] Buss, D M (1989) 'Sex differences in human mate preferences: evolutionary hypotheses testing in 37 cultures', *Behavioral and Brain Sciences*, **12**, pp 1–49

[10] Driscoll, R, Davis, K E and Lipetz, M E (1972) 'Parental interference and romantic love; the Romeo and Juliet effect', *Journal of Personality and Social Psychology*, **24**, pp 1–10

[11] Rubin, Z (1970) 'The measurement of romantic love', *Journal of Personality and Social Psychology*, **16**, pp 265–73

[12] Byrne, D, London, O and Reeves, K (1968) 'The effect of physical attractiveness, sex, and attitude similarity on interpersonal attraction', *Journal of Personality*, **36**, pp 259–71

[13] Nias, D K B (1977) 'Husband-wife similarities', *Social Science*, **52**, pp 206–11

[14] Botwin, M, Buss, D M and Shackelford, T K (1997) 'Personality and mate preferences: five factors in mate selection and marital satisfaction', *Journal of Personality*, **65**, pp 107–36

[15] Eysenck, H J and Wilson, G D (1979) *The Psychology of Sex*, Dent, London

[16] Centers, R (1972) 'The completion hypothesis and the compensatory dynamic in intersexual attraction and love', *The Journal of Psychology*, **82**, pp 111–26

[17] Hahn, J and Blass, T (1977) 'Dating partner preferences: a function of similarity of love styles', *Journal of Social Behavior and Personality*, **12** (3), pp 595–610

[18] Thiessen, D *et al* (1997) 'Social pressures for assortative mating', *Personality and Individual Differences*, **22**, pp 157–64

[19] Kopelman, R E and Lang, D (1985) 'Alliteration in mate selection: does Barbara marry Barry?', *Psychological Reports*, **56**, pp 791–96

[20] Rushton, J P (1989) 'Genetic similarity, human altruism and group selection', *Behavioral and Brain Sciences*, **12**, pp 503–59

[21] Lykken, D T (1993) 'Is human mate selection adventitious or the result of lawful choice? A twin study of mate selection', *Journal of Personality Psychology*, **65**, pp 56–68

## Chapter 4
## The chemistry of love

[1] *Sunday Times Magazine*, 5 October 1999

[2] Money, J (1986) *Lovemaps: Clinical Concepts of Sexual/Erotic Health and Pathology, Paraphilia, and Gender Transposition in Childhood, Adolescence, and Maturity*, Irvington, New York, NY

[3] Liebowitz, M R (1983) *The Chemistry of Love*, Little Brown, Boston, MA

[4] Hess, E (1965) 'Attitude and pupil size', *Scientific American*, **212**, pp 46–54

[5] Carter, C S (1999) 'Neuroendocrine perspectives on social attachment and love', *Psychoendocrinology*, **23**, pp 739–818

[6] Bartels, A and Zeki, S (2000) 'The neural basis of romantic love', *Neuroreport*, **17**, pp 3829–834

[7] Marazziti, D *et al* (1999) 'Alteration of the platelet serotonin transporter in romantic love', *Psychological Medicine*, **29** (3), pp 741–45

[8] Giles, D B (1999) 'Pheromones' effects on sexual attractiveness', Report on London Conference of the British Psychological Society 1998, *The Psychologist*, **12**, pp 123

[9] Grammer, K (1993) 'Andosterone: a male pheromone?', *Ethology and Sociobiology*, **14**, pp 201–07

[10] Cutler, W B, Friedmann, E and McCoy, N L (1998) 'Pheromonal influences on sociosexual behaviour in men', *Archives of Sexual Behavior*, **27**, pp 1–13

[11] See Reference 9

[12] Insel, T R (1992) 'Oxytocin: a neuropeptide for affiliation; evidence for behavioural autoradiographic and comparative studies', *Psychoneuroendocrinology*, **17**, pp 3–35

[13] Fisher, H E (1992) *The Anatomy of Love: The Natural History of Monogamy, Adultery and Divorce*, W W Norton, New York, NY

[14] Porges, S W (1998) 'Love: an emergent property of the autonomic nervous system', *Psychoneuroendocrinology*, **23**, pp 837–61

[15] Insel, T R (1997) 'A neurological basis of social attachment', *American Journal of Psychiatry*, **154**, pp 726–35

[16] Hahn, J and Blass, T (1977) 'Dating partner preferences: a function of similarity of love styles', *Journal of Social Behavior and Personality*, **12** (3), pp 595–610

[17] Komisaruk, B R and Whipple, B (1998) 'Love as sensory stimulation: physiological consequences of its deprivation and expression', *Psychoneuroendocrinology*, **23**, pp 927–44

[18] *Time*, 15 February 1993

[19] Ibid.

## Chapter 5
## Kinds of loving

[1] Bowlby, J (1969) *Attachment and Loss*, Vol I, Basic Books, New York, NY

[2] Bowlby, J (1973) *Attachment and Loss*, Vol II, Basic Books, New York, NY

[3] Shaver, P, Hazan, C and Bradshaw, D (1988) Love as attachment: the integration of three behavioral systems, in *The Psychology of Love*, ed R Sternberg and M Barnes, pp 68–99, Yale University Press, New Haven, CT

[4] Simpson, J A, Rholes, W S and Nelligan, J S (1992) 'Support seeking and support giving within couples in an anxiety-provoking situation: the role of attachment styles', *Journal of Personality and Social Psychology*, **62**, pp 434–46

[5] Simpson, J A (1990) 'Influence of attachment styles on romantic relationships', *Journal of Personality and Social Psychology*, **59**, pp 971–80

[6] McCarthy, G and Taylor, A (1999) 'Avoidant/ambivalent attachment style as a mediator between abusive childhood experiences and adult relationship difficulties', *Journal of Child Psychology and Psychiatry and Allied Disciplines*, **40**, pp 465–77

[7] Lee, J A (1976) *The Colors of Love*, Prentice-Hall, USA

[8] Rubin, Z (1970) *Liking and Loving: An Invitation to Social Psychology*, Holt,

Rinehart and Winston, New York, NY

[9] Sapadin, L A (1988) 'Friendship and gender: perspectives of professional men and women', *Journal of Social and Personal Relationships*, **5**, pp 387–403

[10] Werking, K J (1994) 'Dissolving cross-sex friendships', presented at the Speech Communications Association conference, New Orleans, LA, November

[11] Davies, M F (1996) 'EPQ correlates to love styles', *Personality and Individual Differences*, **20** (2), pp 257–59

[12] Worobey, J (2000) 'Temperament and love attitudes in a college sample', *Journal of Personality and Individual Differences*, in press

[13] Worobey, J (1999) 'Temperament and loving styles in college women: association with eating attitudes', *Psychological Reports*, **84**, pp 305–11

[14] Grote, N K and Frieze, E H (1998) '"Remembrance of things past": perceptions of marital love from its beginnings to the present', *Journal of Social and Personal Relationships*, **15**, pp 91–109

[15] Sprecher, S, Cate, R and Levin, L (1998) 'Parental divorce and young adults' beliefs about love', *Journal of Divorce and Remarriage*, **28** (3–4), pp 107–20

[16] Sternberg, R J and Barnes, M L (1988) *The Psychology of Love*, Yale University Press, New Haven, CT

[17] Aron, A and Westbay, L (1996) 'Dimensions of the prototype of love', *Journal of Personality and Social Psychology*, **70**, pp 535–51

[18] Sternberg, R J (1998) *Cupid's Arrow: The Course of Love Through Time*, Cambridge University Press, New York, NY

[19] Marston, P J *et al* (1998) 'The subjective experience of intimacy, passion and commitment in heterosexual loving relationships', *Personal Relationships*, **5**, pp 15–30

[20] Dion, K K and Dion, K L (1975) 'Self-esteem and romantic love', *Journal of Personality*, **43**, pp 39–57

[21] Dion, K K and Dion, K L (1985) Personality, gender and the phenomenology of romantic love, in *Self, Situations and Behavior: Review of Personality and Social Psychology*, ed P R Shaver, **6**, pp 209–39, Sage, Beverly Hills, CA

[22] Dion, K K and Dion, K L (1988) Romantic love: individual and cultural perspectives, in *The Psychology of Love*, ed R Sternberg and M Barnes, pp 264–89, Yale University Press, New Haven, CT

[23] Hsu, F L K (1981) *Americans and Chinese: Passage to Difference*, 3rd edn, University Press of Hawaii, Honolulu

[24] Hendrick, C and Hendrick, S (1986) 'A theory and method of love', *Journal of Personality and Social Psychology*, **50**, pp 392–402

[25] See Reference 22

[26] Ibid.

[27] Yelsma, P and Athappilly, K (1988) 'Marital satisfaction and communication practices: comparisons among Indian and American couples', *Journal of Comparative Family Studies*, **19**, pp 37–54

[28] Galanter, M (1987) '"Moonies" get married: a psychiatric follow-up study of a charismatic religious sect', *American Journal of Psychiatry*, **143** (10), pp 1245–249

## Chapter 6
## Gender wars

[1] Loyola Management University, Los Angeles

[2] Wiedermann, M W and Allegeier, E R (1994) Male economic status and gender differences in mate selection preferences: evolutionary versus sociocultural explanations, in *Social Stratification and Socioeconomic Inequality*, Vol 2, ed L Ellis, pp 1–12, Praeger, Westport, CT

[3] Hill, R (1945) 'Campus values in mate selection', *Journal of Home Economics*, **37**, pp 554–58

[4] McGinnis, R (1958) 'Campus values in mate selection', *Social Forces*, **35**, pp 368–73

[5] Hudson, J W and Henze, L F (1969) 'Campus values in mate selection: a replication', *Journal of Marriage and the Family*, **31**, pp 772–75

[6] Buss, D M (1989) 'Sex differences in human mate preferences: evolutionary hypotheses testing in 37 cultures', *Behavioural and Brain Sciences*, **12**, pp 1–49

[7] Wiedermann, M W and Allegeier, E R (1992) 'Gender differences in mate selection criteria: sociobiological or socioeconomic explanation?', *Ethology and Sociobiology*, **13**, pp 115–24

[8] 19 August 2000

[9] Buss, D M and Schmitt, D P (1993) 'Sexual strategies theory: an evolutionary perspective on human mating', *Psychological Review*, **100**, pp 204–32

[10] Cameron, C, Oskamp, S and Sparks, W (1978) 'Courtship American-style: newspaper advertisements', *Family Coordinator*, **26**, pp 27–30

[11] Wilson, G D and Nias, D K B (1976) *Love's Mysteries: The Psychology of Sexual Attraction*, Open Books, London

[12] Nevid, J S, Rathus, S A and Rubenstein, H R (1984) *Health in the New Millennium*, Worth Publishers, USA

[13] Hatkoff, T S and Lasswell, T E (1979) Male-female similarities and differences in conceptualising love, in *Love and Attraction: An International Conference*, ed I M Cook and G D Wilson, pp 221–28, Pergamon, Oxford

[14] Wilson, G D and Nias, D K B (1976) *Love's Mysteries: The Psychology of Sexual Attraction*, Open Books, London

[15] Wilson, G D (1997) 'Gender differences in sexual fantasy: an evolutionary analysis', *Personality and Individual Differences*, **22**, pp 27–31

[16] Burrett, J (1993) *Changing Hearts*, Allen and Unwin, London

[17] Wilson, G D (1982) 'Feminism and marital dissatisfaction', *Personality and Individual Differences*, **3**, pp 345–47

[18] Bly, R (1990) *Iron John*, Addison-Wesley, New York, NY

[19] Gray, J (1993) *Men are from Mars, Women are from Venus*, Thorsons, London

[20] Gottman, J M and Levenson, R W (1988) The social psychophysiology of marriage, in *Perspectives on Marital Interaction*, ed P Noller and M A Fitzpatrick, Multilingual Matters, Clevedon, OH and Philadelphia, PA

Chapter 7
Making it last

[1] Office for National Statistics (2000) 'Social Trends', **30**

[2] Family Policy Studies Centre (2000) Lone Parents Report, March

[3] Karney, B R and Bradbury, T N (1995) 'The longitudinal course of marital quality and stability: a review of theory, method and research, *Psychological Bulletin*, **118**, pp 3–34

[4] Riche, M (1988) 'Postmarital society', *American Demographics*, **60**, pp 23–26

[5] Markman, H J (1995) quoted in 'New tools help gauge marital success', R Edwards, *APA Monitor*, February

[6] Kennedy, D (1996) 'How you argue is the key to marital success or failure', *The Times*, 23 October

[7] Patterson, G R and Reid, J B (1970) Reciprocity and coercion: two

facets of social systems, in *Behaviour Modification in Clinical Psychology*, ed C
Neuringer and J Michael, Appleton-Century-Crofts, New York, NY

[8] Gottman, J M (1998) 'Psychology and the study of marital processes',
*Annual Review of Psychology*, **49**, pp 169–97

[9] Gottman, J M (1995) *Why Marriages Succeed or Fail*, Simon and Schuster,
New York, NY

[10] Kingsley, M (1997) 'Get the hell out of a heavenly match', *The Times*, 29
November

[11] Maugh, T H (1998) 'Study's advice to husbands: accept wife's influence',
*Los Angeles Times*, 20 February

[12] Fraenkel, P, Markman, H and Stanley, S (1997) 'The preventive approach
to relationship problems', *Sexual and Marital Therapy*, **12**, pp 249–58

[13] Huston, T L, McHale, S M and Crouter, A C (1986) 'When the
honeymoon's over: changes in the marriage relationship over the first
year', in *The Emerging Field of Personal Relationships*, ed R Gilmour and S
Duck, Erlbaum, Hillsdale, NJ

[14] Sigelman, C K and Shaffer, D R (1995) *Lifespan Human Development*,
Brooks/Cole, New York, NY

[15] Belsky, J, Lang, M E and Rovine, M (1985) 'Stability and change in
marriage across the transition to parenthood: a second study', *Journal of
Marriage and the Family*, **47**, pp 855–65

[16] Cowan, C P *et al* (1991) Becoming a family: marriage, parenting and
child development, in *Family Transitions*, ed P A Cowan and M
Hetherington, Erlbaum, Hillsdale, NJ

[17] Emery, R E and Tuer, M (1993) Parenting and the marital relationship, in
*Parenting: An Ecological Perspective*, ed T L Kuster and L Okagaki, Erlbaum,
Hillsdale, NJ

[18] Rollins, B C and Feldman, H (1970) 'Marital satisfaction over the family
life cycle', *Journal of Marriage and the Family*, **32**, pp 20–28

[19] Solberg, D A, Butler, J and Wagner, N N (1973) 'Sexual behaviour in
pregnancy', *New England Journal of Medicine*, **288**, pp 1098–1103

[20] Myers-Walls, J A (1984) 'Balancing multiple roles and responsibilities
during the transition to parenthood', *Family Relations*, **33**, pp 267–71

[21] Belsky, J (1981) 'Early human experience: a family perspective',
*Developmental Psychology*, **17**, pp 3–23

[22] Kalmuss, D, Davidson, A and Chushman, L (1992) 'Parenting

expectancies, experiences and adjustment to parenthood: a test of the violated expectations framework', *Journal of Marriage and the Family*, **54**, pp 516–26

[23] *The Guardian*, 25 September 2000

[24] Roberts, Y (2000) 'The new divorce', *The Guardian*, 25 September

[25] Ibid.

[26] See Reference 3

[27] Murray, S L, Holmes, J G and Griffin, D W (1996) 'The self-fulfilling nature of positive illusions in romantic relationships. Love is not blind, but prescient', *Journal of Personality and Social Psychology*, **71**, pp 1155–180

Chapter 8
Putting it about

[1] Jung, C (1989) *Memories, Dreams, Reflections*, Vintage, London

[2] Wilson, G D (1981) *Love and Instinct*, Temple Smith, London

[3] Kinsey, A C *et al* (1948) *Sexual Behaviour in the Human Male*, Saunders, Philadelphia, PA

[4] Campbell, A (1989) *The Opposite Sex*, Ebury Press, London

[5] Symons, D (1979) *The Evolution of Human Sexuality*, Oxford University Press, New York, NY

[6] Quoted in *Sunday Telegraph*, 'Every Father's Fear', 19 July 1998

[7] Baker, R and Oram, E (2000) *Baby Wars: Parenthood and Family Strife*, Diane, New York, NY

[8] Dawkins, R (1989) *The Selfish Gene*, Oxford University Press, Oxford

[9] Baker, R (1997) *Sperm Wars: The Evolutionary Logic of Love and Lust*, Basic Books, New York, NY

[10] Short, R V (1979) 'Sexual selection and its component parts: somatic and genital selection as illustrated by man and the great apes', *Advances in the Study of Behaviour*, **9**

[11] Hamer, D H and Copeland, P F (1998) *Living With Our Genes (Why They Matter More Than You Think)*, Doubleday, New York, NY

[12] *The Times*, 1998

[13] *The Sunday Times*, 7 February 1999, 'Genes turn love rats into "monogamice"'

[14] See Reference 6

[15] Baker, R and Bellis, M A (1994) 'Human sperm competition: ejaculate manipulation by females and a function for the female orgasm', *Animal Behaviour*, **46** (5), pp 887–909

[16] Boivin, J et al (1998) University of Cardiff (no other details available)

[17] Enquist, M, Rosenberg, R and Temrin, H (1998) 'The logic of *ménage à trois*', Proceedings of the Royal Society, Ser B 265, pp 609–13

[18] Birkhead, T R (2000) *Promiscuity: An Evolutionary History of Sperm Competition and Sexual Conflict*, Harvard University Press, Boston, MA

[19] Fisher, H (1998) 'Lust, attraction and attachment in mammalian reproduction', *Human Nature*, **9**, pp 23–52

[20] Greiling, H and Buss, D M (2000) 'Women's sexual strategies: the hidden dimension of extra-pair mating', *Journal of Personality and Individual Differences*, **28**, pp 929–63

[21] Hensley, W E (1996) 'The effect of a Ludus love style on sexual experience', *Social Behaviour and Personality*, **24** (3), pp 205–12

[22] Lee, J A (1976) *Lovestyles*, J M Dent, London

[23] Wiedermann, M W and Hurd, C (1999) 'Extradyadic involvement during dating', *Journal of Social and Personal Relationships*, **16** (2), pp 265–74

[24] Drigotas, S M, Safstrom, C A and Gentilia, T (1999) 'An investment model prediction of dating infidelity', *Journal of Personality and Social Psychology*, **77** (3), pp 509–24

[25] Buss, D M and Shackleford, T K (1997) 'Susceptibility to infidelity in the first year of marriage', *Journal of Research in Personality*, **31**, pp 193–221

## Chapter 9
Lovesickness

[1] Grover, J G et al (1985) 'Mate selection processes and marital satisfaction', *Family Relations*, **34**, pp 383–86

[2] Byrne, D and Murnen, S K (1988) 'Maintaining love relationships', in *The Psychology of Love*, Yale University Press, New Haven, CT

[3] Crawford, D W and Huston, T L (1993) 'The impact of the transition to parenthood on marital leisure', *Personality and Social Psychology Bulletin*, **19**, pp 39–46

[4] Andrews, F M, Abbey, A and Halman, L J (1992) 'Stress from infertility: marriage factors and subjective wellbeing of wives and husbands', *Journal of Health and Social Behaviour*, **23**, pp 238–53

⁵ Drigotas, S M and Rusbult, C E (1992) 'Should I stay or should I go? A dependence model of break-ups', *Journal of Personality and Social Psychology*, **62**, pp 62–87

⁶ Baxter, L A (1986) 'Gender differences in the heterosexual relationship rules embedded in break-up accounts', *Journal of Social and Personal Relationships*, **1**, pp 29–48

⁷ Aron, A *et al* (2000) 'Couples' shared participation in novel and arousing activities and experienced relationship quality', *Journal of Personality and Social Psychology*, **78**, pp 273–84

⁸ Rusbult, C E *et al* (1991) 'Accommodation processes in close relationships: theory and preliminary empirical evidence', *Journal of Personality and Social Psychology*, **60**, pp 53–78

⁹ Simpson, J A, Rholes, W S and Phillips, D (1996) 'Conflict in close relationships: an attachment perspective', *Journal of Personality and Social Psychology*, **71**, pp 899–914

¹⁰ Buss, D M *et al* (1992) 'Sex differences in jealousy: evolution, physiology and psychology', *Psychological Science*, **3**, pp 251–55

¹¹ Buunk, B (1984) 'Jealousy as related to attributions for the partner's behaviour', *Social Psychology Quarterly*, **47**, pp 107–12

¹² Buunk, B (1997) 'Personality, birth order and attachment styles as related to various types of jealousy', *Personality and Individual Differences*, **23**, pp 997–1006

¹³ Hill, C T, Rubin, Z and Peplau, L A (1976) 'Break-ups before marriage: the end of 103 affairs', *Journal of Social Issues*, **32** (1), pp 147–68

¹⁴ Harvey, J H, Wells, G L and Alvarez, M D (1978) 'Attribution in the context of conflict and separation in close relationships', in *New Directions in Attribution Research*, Vol 2, ed J H Harvey, W Ickes and R F Kidd, pp 235–60, Erlbaum, Hillsdale, NJ

¹⁵ Wanderer, Z and Cabot, T (1987) *Letting Go: A Twelve-week Personal Action Plan to Overcome a Broken Heart*, Dell, New York, NY

¹⁶ Norwood, R (1986) *Women Who Love Too Much: When You Keep Wishing and Hoping He'll Change*, Pocket Books, New York, NY

¹⁷ British Crime Survey (2000) The Home Office, London

¹⁸ Murray, I (2000) Stalking report, *The Times*, 14 January

¹⁹ Abrams, K M and Robinson, G E (1998) 'Stalking: Part 1: An overview of the problem', *Canadian Journal of Psychiatry*, **43** (5), pp 473–76

[20] Mullen, P E, Pathé, M and Purcell, R (2000) *Stalkers and their Victims*, Cambridge University Press, Cambridge

Chapter 10
In the bedroom

[1] Dahlberg, E (1965) *Reasons of the Heart* (no other details available)

[2] Kelley, K and Musialowski, D (1986) 'Repeated exposure to sexually explicit stimuli: novelty, sex and sexual attitudes', *Archives of Sexual Behaviour*, **15**, pp 487–98

[3] Griffitt, W (1981) Sexual intimacy in aging marital partners, in *Aging: Stability and Change in the Family*, ed J Marsh and S Kiesler, pp 301–15, Academic Press, New York, NY

[4] Ogden, S R and Bradburn, M N (1968) 'Dimensions of marriage happiness', *American Journal of Sociology*, **73**, pp 715–31

[5] Laumann, E O *et al* (1994) *The Social Organization of Sexuality*, University of Chicago Press, Chicago, IL

[6] *The Sun*, 4 September 2000

[7] *The Guardian*, 7 September 2000

[8] Ibid.

[9] Litvinoff, S (1992) *The Relate Guide to Sex in Loving Relationships*, Vermilion, London

[10] Birchler, G R and Webb, L J (1977) 'Discriminating interaction behavior in happy and unhappy marriages', *Journal of Consulting and Clinical Psychology*, **73**, pp 30–37

[11] Smith, E R and Mackie, D M (2000) *Social Psychology*, Psychology Press, Hove, East Sussex

[12] Botwin, M D, Buss, D M and Shackelford, T K (1997) 'Personality and mate preferences: five factors in mate selection and marital preferences', *Journal of Personality*, **65**, pp 107–36

[13] Hulbert, D F, Apt, C V and White, L C (1992) 'An empirical examination into the sexuality of women with borderline personality disorder', *Journal of Sex and Marital Therapy*, **18**, pp 231–42

[14] Howard, J W and Dawes, R M (1976) 'Linear prediction of marital happiness', *Personality and Social Psychology Bulletin*, **2**, pp 478–80

[15] Frank, B, Dixon, D M and Gross, H J (1993) 'Conjoint monitoring of symptoms of premenstrual syndrome: impact on marital satisfaction',

*Journal of Counselling Psychology,* **40**, pp 109–14

[16] May 2000

[17] Rix, J (1995) *Is There Sex After Childbirth?,* Thorsons, London

[18] Pallas, J *et al* (2000) 'A study using Viagra in a mental health practice', *Journal of Sex and Marital Therapy,* **26** (1), pp 41–50

[19] Nurnberg, H G *et al* (1999) 'Sildenafil for women patients with anti-depressant-induced sexual dysfunction', *Psychiatric Services,* **50** (8), pp 1076–78

[20] Lang, A R (1985) 'The social psychology of drinking and human sexuality', *Journal of Drug Issues,* **15** (2), pp 273–89

[21] Weller, A and Halikas, J A (1984) 'Marijuana use and sexual behaviour', *Journal of Sex Research,* **20** (2), pp 186–93

[22] Sternbach, H (1998) 'Age-associated testosterone decline in men: clinical issues', *American Journal of Psychiatry,* **155** (10), pp 1310–318

[23] Warnock, J K *et al* (1999) 'Female hypoactive sexual disorder: case studies of physiologic androgen replacement', *Journal of Sex and Marital Therapy,* **25** (3), pp 175–82

## Chapter 11
## Hope over experience

[1] Wylie, M P (1999) 'The experience of successful couples' relationships: a heuristic exploration', Dissertation Abstracts International: Section B, *The Sciences and Engineering,* **60** (1-B), 0414

[2] Ceglian, C P and Gardner, S (1999) 'Attachment style: a risk for multiple marriage?', *Journal of Divorce and Remarriage,* **31** (1–2), pp 125–39

[3] Grizzle, G L (1996) 'Remarriage as an incomplete institution: Cherlin's (1978) views and why we should be cautious about accepting them', *Journal of Divorce and Remarriage,* **26**, pp 191–201

[4] Hagestad, G O and Smyer, M A (1982) 'Dissolving long-term relationships: patterns of divorcing in middle age', in *Personal Relationships 4: Dissolving Personal Relationships,* ed S W Duck, Academic Press, London

[5] Talbot, M M (1998) 'Older widows' attitudes towards men and remarriage', *Journal of Aging Studies,* **12** (4), pp 429–49

[6] Stark, E (1986) 'Friends through it all', *Psychology Today,* **20** (5), pp 54–60

[7] Buunk, B P and Mutsaers, W (1999) 'The nature of the relationship between remarried individuals and former spouses and its impact on

# References

marital satisfaction', *Journal of Family Psychology*, **13** (2), pp 165–74

[8] Wineberg, H (1997) 'Association between having a failed marital reconciliation in the first marriage and dissolution of the second marriage', *Journal of Divorce and Remarriage*, **27** (3–4), pp 39–50

[9] Buunk, B P and Mutsaers, W (1999) 'Equity perceptions and marital satisfaction in former and current marriage', *Journal of Social and Personal Relationships*, **16** (1), pp 123–32

[10] Sullivan, O (1997) 'The division of housework among "remarried" couples', *Journal of Family Issues*, **18** (2), pp 205–23

[11] Prado, L M and Markham, H J (1999) 'Unearthing the seeds of marital distress: what we have learned from married and unmarried couples', in *Conflict and Cohesion in Families: Causes and Consequences*, ed M J Cox *et al*, Lawrence Erlbaum Associates Inc., Hillsdale, NJ

[12] Glick, P C and Lin, S (1986) 'Recent changes in divorce and remarriage', *Journal of Marriage and the Family*, **48** (4), pp 737–47

[13] Lampard, R and Peggs, K (1999) 'Repartnering: the relevance of parenthood and gender to cohabitation and remarriage among the formerly married', *British Journal of Sociology*, **50** (3), pp 443–65

[14] Cherlin, A J *et al* (1991) 'Longitudinal studies of effects of divorce on children in Great Britain and the United States', *Science*, **252**, pp 1386–389

[15] Isaacs, M B and Leon, G H (1988) 'Remarriage and its alternatives following divorce: mother and child adjustments', *Journal of Marital and Family Therapy*, **14**, pp 163–73

[16] Cargan, L and Melko, M (1982) *Singles: Myths and Realities*, Sage Publications, Beverly Hills and London

[17] Lewis, K G and Moon, S (1997) 'Always single and single again women: a qualitative study', *Journal of Marital and Family Therapy*, **23** (2), pp 115–34

[18] Mannis, V S (1999) 'Single mothers by choice', *Family Relations*, **48**, pp 121–28

# Index

# Index

# Index

# Other books from Fusion

## The Book of the Penis
Maggie Paley

The penis is an object of adoration, revulsion, ridicule, joy, pride and frustration. But does anyone fully understand the penis? Maggie Paley immerses herself in the world of this most forthright of organs. She pores over anthropology texts and sex-shop glossies, and interviews sex workers and transsexuals. She even objectively addresses the big question: 'Does size matter?'

The reader encounters entertaining and informative chapters on circumcision, castration, fellatio, the role of the penis in art, fashion, literature, films and much more. Revealing truths and insights from ancient Greece to modern-day cyberspace, the author separates fact from fiction.

Interspersed with humorous illustrations, this compelling book opens up a universal subject to women and men, gay and straight, in an accessible and light-hearted way, without being lewd or crude.

£9.99
ISBN: 1-901250-78-4

## Self Sexual Healing – Finding Pleasure Within
Jo-Anne Baker

*Self Sexual Healing* shows that everyone has the power to find sexual pleasure. Through a combination of ancient wisdom, modern psychology and relaxation and energising techniques, author Jo-Anne Baker explores sexual blocks, fears and inhibitions, and prescribes simple, tried-and-tested techniques to release them forever.

Practical exercises and tips include erotic massage, fantasy, striptease and sensual exploration and can be easily used whether single or in a relationship.

*Self Sexual Healing* answers such questions as: How do I achieve amazing orgasms? How important is masturbation? Where is the G-spot? What are the best sex toys to use?

Jo-Anne Baker shows that the individual is the key to their own sexual happiness; nobody has to wait for the perfect partner to have the best sex. *Self Sexual Healing* shows that sexuality is a lifelong adventure, one that can be fun and dynamic. Sexuality can be explored alone or in a relationship, making each person empowered and happy in the process.

£9.99
ISBN: 1-901250-67-9

## Sex Herbs – Nature's Sexual Enhancers for Men and Women

Beth Ann Petro Roybal and Gayle Skowronski

As patients rush to try expensive pharmaceutical medicines, few realise that nature already provides safe ways to boost sexual desire, pleasure and fulfilment. *Sex Herbs* offers natural alternatives from around the world to enhance the sex lives of both men and women.

The authors address lovemaking from a holistic perspective, recognising that one's emotional and physical health will inevitably affect the libido. Divided into specific topic areas, *Sex Herbs* makes it easy to find herbs that help with many sexual issues: to stimulate desire, to make lovemaking more pleasurable, to compensate for hormonal changes such as menopause or premenstrual tension. Impotence and general stress-related health conditions are also covered; the book shows how to reduce tension for a better sex life.

Featuring over 60 herbs in detail, the authors show how plants have been used historically and in today's societies. Profiling safe, available herbs, this book is essential reading for anyone wishing to enhance their sex life in a natural and holistic way.

£9.99
ISBN: 1-901250-62-8

## Sex Tips – From Women Who Ride the Sexual Frontier
Edited by Jo-Anne Baker

A remarkable collection from female sexual pioneers who span the globe, *Sex Tips* describes women at the fore of a new sexual revolution. Women from wildly different backgrounds give hints and advice on subjects ranging from exhibitionism and sex toys to performance art, fetishism and gender bending.

With entries from Annie Sprinkle, Susie Bright and Joani Blank, amongst others, *Sex Tips* details women who are experts in their field, alongside women who simply have a refreshing outlook on sex. Editor Jo-Anne Baker shows that sex can be exciting in and out of a relationship. In a relationship sex is like glue; it can strengthen a couple when things go well, or smooth over the rougher times. Sex when you're single can be fulfilling, exciting and enriching.

*Sex Tips* is a must for any woman, anyone who knows a woman, would like to be a woman, or for couples wanting to spice up their love life. Whether or not you want to ride the sexual frontier, *Sex Tips* is a unique and erotic account of those who do.

£9.99
ISBN: 1-901250-73-3

All Vision Paperbacks and Fusion Press titles are available from good bookshops.

Alternatively, you can place an order for our titles with our distributor, Orca Book Services:

Tel:        01202 665432
Fax:       01202 666219
e-mail:   orders@orcabookservices.co.uk

We are always interested in hearing from prospective authors and like-minded publishers worldwide. Please write to:

Vision Paperbacks
101 Southwark Street
London
SE1 0JH
UK